ADVANCE PRAISE FOR
The Honest Backpacker

The Honest Backpacker lays out essential hiking details in an organized, easy read. More important, it imparts a philosophy of walking that will stay for a lifetime. It will do the same for any hiker, especially the aging walker, and give them the stoke to start their next adventure.

—MALCOLM DALY, *Neptune Mountaineering*,
Boulder, Colorado

The Honest Backpacker is a step-by-step guide for anyone just starting or needing a refresher course on the intricacies of backpacking. Klopovic intersperses trail tales from his experiences that add humor and interest to the facts. His book does not miss a step.

—AUDREY TOWNSEND, Outfitter and Owner,
Townsend Bertram and Company,
Carrboro, North Carolina

A well written and thorough guide to making the most of your adventure on the trail. See you out there!

—RON and ANNE HOUSER, owners of *The Mountain Goat*,
Outdoor Specialty Retailer on the AT/LT,
Manchester Center, Vermont

I believe the trail is there for everyone, at every phase of life, however, the more mature hiker is often overlooked, especially if they are new to backpacking. *The Honest Backpacker* fills a much-needed void with vivid anecdotes and practical step-by-step instructions for folks over the age of 50 who are hitting the trail for the first time.

— JENNIFER PHARR DAVIS, Author, Speaker and
National Geographic Adventurer of the Year

The Honest Backpacker

A Practical Guide for the Rookie Adventurer over 50

**JAMES KLOPOVIC
& NICOLE KLOPOVIC**

AFFINITAS PUBLISHING
Morrisville, NC

AFFINITAS PUBLISHING

The Honest Backpacker: A Practical Guide for the Rookie Adventurer over 50

First Edition, 2017
Copyright © 2017 James Klopovic

Publisher
Affinitas Publishing
A division of Affinitas LLC
208 Courthouse Drive
Morrisville, NC 27560
HonestBackpacker.com

For interview, excerpts, or permission requests, email
hikewiththeHB@gmail.com.

ISBN: 978-0-9982372-0-6 (Print)
ISBN: 978-0-9982372-1-3 (e-Readers)

Editor and Project Manager: Marla Markman, www.MarlaMarkman.com
Cover and Interior Design: Kelly Cleary
Cover Photo: Chris Hoina Sr.
Photographs and Illustrations: As noted or by author

All rights reserved. No part of this publication may be reproduced, distributed, or transmitted in any form or by any means, including photocopying, recording, or other electronic or mechanical methods, without the prior written permission of the publisher, except in the case of brief quotations embodied in critical reviews and certain other noncommercial uses permitted by copyright law. For permission requests, write to the publisher, addressed "Attention: Permissions Coordinator," at the address above.

Publisher's Cataloging-in-Publication Data

Names: Klopovic, James, author | Klopovic, Nicole, author.

Title: The honest backpacker : a practical guide for the rookie adventurer over 50/ James Klopovic, D.P.P. and Nicole Klopovic, PA-C.

Description: Includes bibliographical references and index. | Morrisville, NC: Affinitas LLC, 2017.

Identifiers: ISBN 978-0-9982372-0-6 (pbk.) | 978-0-9982372-1-3 (e-book) | LCCN 2016917698

Subjects:
LCSH Backpacking–United States. | Hiking for older people. | Baby boom generation–Recreation.
BISAC SPORTS & RECREATION / Hiking.

Classification: LCC GV199.53.K56 2017 | DDC 796.51084/6--dc23

Printed in the United States of America
21 20 19 18 17 / 10 9 8 7 6 5 4 3 2 1

To Nicole, Cindy, and Carolyn

In equal measure, each immeasurable in your own way,

let your heart tell your feet where to take you.

Acknowledgments

Acknowledging all who made this book possible would be impossible. There is much to be said about giving credit where credit is due; however, an honest listing of contributors would surely dwarf the space allotted. When pursuing the outdoors, so many acquaintances, like those below, become lifelong friends. These people, good, dear friends all, have each given me remarkable life moments, along with the honor of calling them *friend*.

Anson Byrd, gentleman, good ol' boy, politician and friend, who knew more about hunting and fishing and nature than most anyone you could meet. You are still an inspiration to me and many others. Your picture taken on the Bighorn River watches over me now. We miss you, Anson.

Burt Kornegay, the consummate wilderness guide who introduced me to the outdoors and how to do it well. I can still hear you reciting the "Scat" poem over a pile of bear evidence on the trail.

Don "Marty" Martin, my dear, dear friend since basic training now these more than 50 years. When life's blood left me, you found it for me and keep it to this day.

Bob Peoples of Kincora Hiking Hostel: A trip to the woods is worth any expense and effort just to listen to your stories.

Wes Riffle, "Mr. 99," who arranged for me to stay an extra week in England on the Coast-to-Coast hike. I will always remember the best haircut I ever got and an even better home brew.

Robert "Bobby" Rupert, who showed me how to be a true friend, a Southern gentleman, and what a good BBQ and a good dog really are. So few are as good as Sid. Here's to raisin' good grandchildren and dogs.

Glen Swicegood, who showed me more life moments in the outdoors than just about anyone. I can still see the triple in Montana! Nothing like being in the ol' Hewes with you, Glen!

CONTENTS

Acknowledgments	VI
PREFACE	1
INTRODUCTION	3
The *Honest Backpacker* Evolves	4
The Who, What, When, Where and How of It	5
ROI: There Is Much More for You Than a Hike	7
PART I: PREPARATION	**11**
CHAPTER 1	
Create a Timeline	13
Preparation Overview	14
CHAPTER 2	
Milestones at a Glance	19
Decide Where and When to Hike	19
Research or Reconnoiter Trailheads	20
Conduct Initial Meeting of Hikers	21
Complete Medical Profile and Physical	23
Begin Physical Conditioning	23
Begin Better Diet	24
Reserve Accommodations	24
Attend Classes (If Available)	24
Procure Gear—Backpack First	25
Train in Gear	26
Do a Short Overnight Shakedown Trip	26
Ramp Up the Physical Training	27
Procure Food	27
Procure Any Prescription Medications	27
Plan Post-Trip Debrief/Critique	28
Attend to Personal Affairs During the Trip	28
Confirm Accommodations and Determine Trail Conditions	29
Check Weather	29
Consider Leaving the Cell Phone Behind	29
Pack	29
Hit the Trail	30
Conduct Post-Trip Debrief/Critique	30
Discuss Ideas/Plan Next Trip	30

PART II: THE WHOLE PERSON 35

CHAPTER 3
Introduction to the Whole Person 37
What Is "The Whole Person"? 38
Body: Establish a Physical Fitness Regimen 38
Mind: Investigate Mindfulness 39
Spirit: Getting "Up" for the Trip 40
Set Realistic Expectations 40
It's All in Your Mind 41

CHAPTER 4
Getting Yourself Ready: Physical Fitness 43
Discipline, Diet and Common Sense 45
Three Simple Rules 45
Diet Attitude 46
The 40-30-30 Plan 52
Getting Through the Day: A Daily Schedule of Meals 54
Getting in Shape for Boomers 56
What Kind of Exercise Are We Talking About? 56
Make Exercise a Habit 59
Exercise Tips from Olympians 60
Exercise Intelligently 62
What Is a Boomer to Do? 62
Doing Resistance Exercises Sensibly 65
A Week of Exercise: An Example 67
Dealing With Setbacks 69
Milestones for the Run-Up to the Hike 71
One Year Out: Put the Whole-Person Plan in Place 71
Six Months Out: Throw in a Little Prep for Actual Hiking 72
Three Months Out: Transition to Actual Hiking 72
Six Weeks Out: Get Trail-Hardened Before You Have To 73

CHAPTER 5
Getting Yourself Ready: Mental Fitness 75
General Knowledge and Education 76
Technical Skills 76
When Enough Is Enough 79
A Word About Your Sawbones (Seeing a Doctor, That Is) 79

CHAPTER 6
Getting Yourself Ready: A Fit Spirit   83

PART III: PACKING ESSENTIALS   87

CHAPTER 7
Gear   89
- *Essential and Optional Gear*   91
  - The Backpack   92
  - Sleeping: To Tent or Not to Tent?   93
  - Getting Ready to Eat: Fire, Pot and Spoon   95
  - Hydration   99
  - Clothing: Lightweight and Just Enough   100
  - First Aid: All That Will Fit in a Plastic Baggie   105
  - General Camp Equipment and Repairs   107
  - Toiletries and Toilet: There Is a Difference   108
  - Orienteering and Daily Journal Logging   110
  - Miscellaneous   112
- *Ignore This Advice at Your Peril*   114

CHAPTER 8
Food   117
- *A Matter of Perspective*   118
- *Menu Planning*   119
- *Convenient But Nutritious*   120
- *Keeping Fueled From "Me" and "You"*   121
  - Eating Equipment   122
  - Meals   123
- *Personalize It: Your Pack Is Yours*   124

PART IV: HITTING THE TRAIL   129

CHAPTER 9
Trail-Tested Wisdom from The Honest Backpacker   131
- Tip 1: Stop and Smell the Jasmine   132
- Tip 2: Check Hiking Conditions Around Starting Time   132
- Tip 3: Assemble Gear   133
- Tip 4: Plan Transportation to and From the Hike   133

Tip 5: Get the Most Out of Your Hike	135
Tip 6: Bone Up on Trail Nutrition	139
Tip 7: Learn How to Set Up and Break Camp Efficiently	141
Tip 8: Practice Good Safety, Health and Hygiene	143
Tip 9: Have a Plan B	145

CHAPTER 10
Correcting Errata — 149

AFTERWORD
Perspectives of an Experienced Hiker — 155

Appendix 1
Leave No Trace: Outdoor Ethics — 157

Appendix 2
Adult Medical Information for The Trail — 160

Appendix 3
Authorization and Consent Form — 161

Appendix 4
Adult Medical History — 162

Resources — 163

Photo Credits — 169

About the Authors — 170

Index — 171

PREFACE

You know, of all the stuff we have read, none of it really helps the older hiker, especially us boomers. What we need is an Honest Backpacker, words of wisdom for the rest of us.
—Crackerjack

Laurel Falls on the Appalachian Trail

As life would have it, after two careers, children and a little education, where I was so busy that I didn't have time to write a bucket list, let alone do one, and had to say no to many wonderful, wild and memorable things, I finally did something memorable. I had a chance to reinvent myself, take a bit better care of myself and make memories. I said yes to just about everything—things most people only dream about—as long as it was legal, healthy, fun and done with interesting people.

So, well into my 50s, when people asked, "Jim, would you like to travel?" I said, "Yes." Jim, would you like to make new friends? Yes. Jim, would you like to do a triathlon? Yes. But please let it be a sprint at a gentlemanly pace. Would you like to learn to make apple pie and win the grand prize blue ribbon? Did that too (you should have seen the faces on the women who thought their prize was stolen from them—by a man, no less.) Jim, would you like to learn to shoot skeet? Oh, yeah. Jim, would you like to write a couple of books?

Here's the first, and more are in the works. Would you like to do a little hunting and fishing? Count me in. Jim, would you like to go back to school and earn a doctorate? Yes. Even though I quit a couple of times, as it was much like dropping an anvil on your toes. How about becoming a better, more interesting person and have like friends? Yup. Do you think you can find the love of your life? That happened too—just like high school, only better. Jim, would you like to go on a couple of fantastic hikes? Hell, yes!

Saying yes to things has made all the difference. I have retired and become a cliché. I am much busier now than I was when slogging through those two careers. But thanks to saying yes, I am in fantastic health for my age, enough to continue growing, adventuring and making memories. Being a senior citizen, with a little discretionary money, a good set of teeth, a full head of hair and most of my marbles, retirement is all it should be. I highly recommend it.

It is with this "yes" frame of mind that I decided to do a little hiking. I read about the England Coast-to-Coast hike in *Smithsonian* magazine. Offered as a guided adventure, at a *"Smithsonian* price," it motivated me to take the DIY route. As it turned out, all the information I needed to help me prepare was on the web. Plus, organizing and planning is one of my things. I ran the family farm at 16, and my Air Force career was as a logistician.

There was much I needed to find out about this backpacking idea. As is my habit, I kept notes—lots of them. I had to. There was so much to learn, and very little was available on how a baby boomer should proceed. Most of the information seemed to expect a basic knowledge of hiking and was written by younger authors who assumed readers arrived to the task in great shape and bulletproof. The pile of notes grew in topical stacks and seemed to say, "Write me into a book."

So here you have an honest backpacker whose only concern is sharing a few tips and tales from the trail. So, the journey continues . . .

INTRODUCTION

There is everything right about spending a day in the woods, on a river, or cooking weenies with a child over an open fire if you suspect you have a mind to do it. It is worth the effort. Plan for a good experience, and it will happen— over and over again.
—James Klopovic

Because flowers say it all

At 3,500 feet in the Tennessee Appalachians, with sweat on our brows and hyperventilating between glimpses of impossible beauty, my longtime hiking buddy, Crackerjack, planted the seed for a book on the outdoors for the older and inexperienced hiker. We lamented there is little information on hiking for the older adventurer and a need to explain the fundamentals, especially backpacking, for the boomer generation because there are so many of us, and more than a few who aspire to do things we have never done before and have no idea how to go about them[1].

---

[1] A baby boomer is anyone who remembers singing Beatles tunes when they were still together while walking to elementary school. You know who you are by those memories— and the achy joints.

The Honest Backpacker Evolves

How do you write something for the seasoned boomer that is purposeful, succinct and enjoyable to read? It would be nice if others in search of an outdoor experience found some helpful advice also. It was an obvious and rather large hole in the bookstore that needed to be filled. We boomers have age-appropriate needs, for goodness' sake! Many of us expect to be vigorous into our 90s and want to make the most of it but do it safely and with as little pain—physical and mental—as possible.

> **"Many of us expect to be vigorous into our 90s and want to make the most of it but do it safely and with as little pain—physical and mental—as possible."**

We boomers continue to experiment with and change how life is lived. We can make the time if we want. Many of us have the money. And we have the dreams to pretty much do what we can—*can* being the operative word. We are also very aware that we are on "the short rows" and want to make the most of what we have left. The reality is that it takes longer now to heal from injury. Let's face it: Flying a desk for 40 or more years is hard but sedentary work. Anything physical, especially something as demanding as backpacking, must be approached with great care, preparation and concern if there is to be a hike at all, let alone subsequent experiences.

Getting ready for a hike is no easy task for any would-be hiker, especially those approaching and rebelling against their "golden" years. Yet most "how to" literature seems to assume the intrepid gray-haired hiker is in a perpetual state of readiness. It is assumed (and sometimes attempted) that we can strap on a backpack full of hearth and home, including a bladder of Chianti, and knock off a 15-mile, uphill day hike (I can personally attest to the folly of this idea). The mature hiker thinks, acts, perceives and moves differently from a 20- or even a 50-something! For example, we all have six-pack abs; they just come in one container and are most times supersized.

That is but one indication that we have a lot of work ahead to prepare for any outdoor experience, let alone one of substance, length and meaning. We need to know how to get ready by preparing just enough to reasonably ensure a good, safe, fun experience in enough abundance to want to do it again.

Preparing for anything physical, especially after having grown up as the first TV generation, *must* be a whole-body, whole-person experience, well in advance of the happy event. For some, this could mean a year or two of planned, progressive preparation. We have to gradually but relentlessly work toward comfortably doing an hour of good, conscientious, hard physical conditioning at least five times per week. Conditioning must consider flexibility, core, balance, aerobic and anaerobic exercising in that order, and all done respecting the needs and capabilities of a mature person—say, beyond 50 years old. We must educate ourselves in the general knowledge and technical skills of being in the woods, or risk dining on tree bark soufflé just before the big final hike in the sky. Even more important than being physically and technically ready, we must remain excited about any endeavor out of the ordinary; part of a life worth living is dreaming and making a few of those dreams happen.

The Who, What, When, Where, and How of It

My goal with this book is to cut through the volumes of clutter and information out there, organizing the most essential advice on getting ready into one document, and then put the information into an easily understood, logical process and format. I want to make sure the mature adventurer can have a safe, enjoyable and memorable experience—and want to do it again.

Although I tried not to duplicate what you can quickly learn from other sources, references and face-to-face conversations with other backpacking enthusiasts, when researching your own hike, I encourage you to explore as far and wide as your need and curiosity take you.

A good goal is to prepare your own body of knowledge by reading this book, augmenting it with internet searches and organizing a personal binder that takes you through the whole process. Speaking of processes, I suggest following the book's chapters in order because it follows an organized method, whether you're getting ready for a weekend of car camping with children a few yards from your back door or a wilderness backpacking expedition.

Who can benefit from *The Honest Backpacker*? While it is written from the blissfully ignorant perspective of an eager and unaware baby boomer who needs complete preparation, anyone who wishes to hike, even for a day, can find useful information in these pages. This book will take a wanderer through preparation of their body, mind and soul; get them outfitted and provisioned for a good experience; and get them back with a reasonable assurance that the experience will be done well and memorably. Likewise, a family with young children who wishes to "hike" 100 yards from the car and pitch a tent will also be prepared. In fact, one of my hopes is that if the youngest of adventurers returns from the hike with a good, even giddy experience, they will do it for a lifetime. They will also learn life lessons, as they may be invited to help get ready for an outing. Even toting their own backpack filled with some necessities and a favorite blanket will resonate for years.

The book is laid out in a logical progression of preparing to hit the trail, a little of what to expect on the trail, and returning wanting more. By avoiding discouragement and career-ending mistakes on the first hiking attempt, we hope you will leap at a chance for a second hike.

We boomers appreciate easy reading; hence, where I could, I put things into a checklist or bulleted format, organized by the logical sequence of getting ready for a venture into the woods. The lame attempts at humor are my fault; the humor that works is to the credit of others. I also added a little flavor and seasoning via anecdotes and vignettes from the trail; every adventure needs to be retold.

Also, to add a little spice and enticement to the book, I have included several sections, commonly called stages, from the journal I kept when hiking across northern England on the England Coast-to-Coast (C2C) hike. It is one of the most popular, and to me most spectacular, hikes on the planet. Every turn created a lifetime memory for me. I hope that getting a little taste of the trail will motivate you to give it a try. You can do a few day hikes, take a sponsored trip or tackle the whole thing. But do refer to *The Honest Backpacker*.

I want to realistically prepare you while encouraging you to get your feet and soul surrounded by earth, wind and nature. I am aware that many prospective hikers, whether they want to day hike with a grandchild or backpack for any length of time, don't know where to begin. For that reason, *The Honest Backpacker* is written from the perspective of the first-time mature hiker. However, it's not limited to that group. This book will address the needs of anyone who wishes to get on the trail and into nature. Even for a one-day hike at a local park, the reader will find it useful to cruise through the whole book and then return to it when needed.

With this basic and complete volume, you'll be ready to hit the trail at the literal drop of a hat. My equipment is lined up on hangers in a closet, ready to hike the Milford Track in New Zealand, the number-one hike in the world, or head to the local park. You will be prepared to go anywhere reasonable—*reasonable* being the operative word. Let me be clear: This book will not prepare you to climb Mount Everest, but it will get you ready for experiences that will tell you if you are ready for more challenging treks. And you will gain the basic knowledge and confidence to step out in various ways. Organizing and preparing for a hike has also made me quite competent to prepare for trout fishing and grouse hunting in Wyoming, bone-fishing in Belize, and going for a walkabout in Australia. So, get a great pair of ankle-height, lightweight hiking boots; a broad-brimmed hat; and a set of hiking poles, and break them in.

ROI: There Is Much More for You Than a Hike

Getting out and about is indeed the road less traveled and the means to many other ends. Throughout these pages there are chances to reflect on where such a path leads; the opportunities are just about limitless. If it is better health you seek, you shall have it. If you want a daily diet of natural beauty, it's there. If you want to experience the honest camaraderie born of sweat, pain and companionship, it only takes a few days buried in God's woods or along His river with a hiking buddy. If you need a little therapy, there is nothing like the silent sounds of a primitive forest. You *will* understand yourself and others better. Even your media-tainted and life-tattered opinion of your fellow man will be greatly improved by the actualization of personal achievement and the subsequent desire to reach out to others, but more so by the very large amounts of humanity, friendliness, cheerfulness and neighborliness that come by way of a simple footpath. Folks on the trail are just interesting, friendly and giving.

It is astonishing how human and humane people on the trail are. Few places are safer than in your tent at 4,500 feet. You will meet extraordinary and, occasionally, wonderfully goofy people and make instant friends with whom to share a shelter. In any other circumstance, you wouldn't dare raise an eyelid to such people; here, all that is needed is a chance meeting on common ground. The trail is a great leveler of life's playing field. Your Christmas card list will grow exponentially if you want it to. Every hike, no matter how modest, produces a trail legend or two, and that is a good thing. You may even be one of them. The people you meet are the stuff of life.

The pursuit of this type of adventure is not only a lifestyle change, but it is lifestyle betterment, which involves body, mind and soul. Even a short hike of a few days is motivation enough to actually lose a few pounds and drive past instead of through the Golden Starches. Imagine the day you can look down and happily see your toes and other appendages after a hiatus of about 20 years and an advanced case of "Abdominal Diaspora." This book is a guide to prepare you for a hike, to do the hike, and want to do it again. While *The Honest Backpacker* is a complete guide, it is also an introduction to spark your interest in investigating further; there is so much to read, see and do before, during and after a hike (or any life experience that will grow from a hike). The study of the trail is fascinating; there is something primal about it. After all, we as Homo sapiens were built and programmed to walk. If we weren't, we'd be worms.

Throughout the book, we may merely refer to a source, which you may pursue for a better and more thorough elaboration of the point in question. The reference list is purposely brief. If you want padded and useless bibliographies, please take a graduate course in anything. Besides, backpacking is not that difficult, though "prepared must you be" (I think Yoda said that).

Record things! Build a modest library of your own making. And be sure you have an album of actual photos going, not just those on an iPhone that could be lost to the family on some kind of cloud thingy. Also, note that you can put other things in an album besides pictures; how about that piece of duct tape you had on your heel for 10 days, the one with shreds of meat still stuck to it? (OK, maybe not.)

Write in a journal, every day, even moment by moment as the mood and muse strike. Benjamin Franklin said it best, "Either write things worth reading or do things worth the writing." Even the smallest written observation or sketch can bring back floods of memories. Just be sure to chronicle your trip, be it through a journal, memorabilia, quotes from trail sages, scraps of things from the trail, a preserved flower, pictures or all these things. Once started, it is happily never-ending. Someone, sometime will be interested in knowing who you are, what you did, and how you did it. What a glorious thing if it is a grandchild who is inspired to ask you to take them camping!

> **Benjamin Franklin said it best,**
> **"Either write things worth reading or do things worth the writing."**

At the risk of being trite, if ever you make an excursion off the couch—*just do it*. But do so in an organized, cautious and resolute way. The side benefits are nothing short of enormous: enjoying better health, meeting wonderful people, finding exotic places and interesting things. Perhaps you will discover a little more self-awareness and faith in your neighbor, or maybe even dream a few more dreams to make happen. Go ahead: Plan a hike across England or a trek in Nepal with Sherpas and yaks; do the Milford Track in New Zealand; backpack to a remote river in Alaska for the salmon run and have a glorious dinner of the day's catch by the river (away from the bears); hike through Sicily to help with the grape harvest, pay a visit to a newly made trail friend, and bring your journal.

Take a moment, right now, to dream your own dream. And get with it before you really do get too old. If you want to hike a remote trout stream, do it—just bring a fry pan, some Cajun spices and a little canola oil. It's amazing how useless a TV remote really is and how divine peanut butter in a tortilla can be. Is it too corny to say again that it is, after all, the little things, the things *anyone* can have, that make all the difference?

Whatever adventures you may have or are planning, please heat up some ramen with me at the next shelter, and let me hear all about it.

PART I: PREPARATION

In all things of nature there is something of the marvelous.
—Aristotle

Any ol' stream in England—one of scores on the Coast-to-Coast hike

There is nothing like a timeline to put an idea on the road to happening. This is where the dreaming ends and the doing begins. By writing down what you need to do, it is a simple matter to add, subtract and modify on the fly. Hikers understand what they must do and when it is helpful to have it done. The timeline also doubles as a meeting agenda if your hike is a group effort and makes any get-together more efficient and meaningful; there is a sense of moving ahead. During this period of gathering information and preparation, confidence is building. You know you will be ready for the trail, have fun and return safely. And when something is accomplished, it can be checked off the bucket list with a flourish.

The milestones listed assume that you are starting from zero—that is, you are out of shape, don't know where to start and may not be all that certain a hike in the woods is a good idea (don't worry, it is). Each milestone suggests a to-do list of its own, which are pretty much the essential activities for your hike. Taken together, they outline a campaign of sorts, and as much as possible ensure a good result. The milestones improve your learning curve because they are a proven way to do things. There is no muddling around or wild mongoose chases unless you want an occasional side pursuit. After some experience, you can take the milestone checklist and modify it to your needs, skills and hike of the moment.

CHAPTER 1
Create a Timeline

Less is really *more.*
—James Klopovic

A kissing gate to keep sheep from straying on the England Coast-to-Coast hike

When preparing for a trip, you will find that you will be either maddeningly obsessive or entirely too casual. Our aim is to get you somewhere in the middle for your sake and for those who must put up with you as you get ready. Even if your usual hike is a round-robin of the local mall, which likely means your first adventure may be spending just one night in the outdoors, you very well may go overboard. You will imagine everything that can possibly go wrong or right and plan as if you were Rome preparing to meet the Hun. Then there are those who have blind faith that they can pack a few things and "get in shape on the trail." Neither of these is correct, obviously.

So, start with a plan—and make it *your* plan; it would be a great compliment to me if you do. The preparation in *The Honest Backpacker* is for a shorter hike of around a week, just enough to do a wilderness backpacking experience of 50 miles or more and spend five to six days on the trail. Lessons learned and equipment bought and trail tested then translate to just about any hike, even if it is to do the whole Appalachian Trail (AT).

Preparation Overview

Let me introduce you to trip planning à la backpacking. As the title of this section suggests, this is a brief overview to get your ball rolling. More details follow in the rest of *The Honest Backpacker*.

It's beneficial to have as complete a timeline of milestones as possible. To do that, take the "Hiker's Timeline of Milestones" provided on page 17 and personalize it depending on your adventure and preparation requirements.

One thing about taking the time to keep documentation is that the stuff worth chronicling grows in volume, purpose and meaning as you do. Someone, sometime will want to know how you passed through this life; hopefully a future grandchild. Furthermore, it is much more thorough than that steel trap we once had for a mind. Once complete, you will use it over and over again. A mile high and drenched in sweat is no time to realize you packed your pills in the street clothes bag back in the SUV.

Like all good construction projects, preparing for a night on the trail is labor-intensive, especially the first time, but the better the plan, the better the building, and once done, the next trip goes a whole lot faster. The reality is when you start with a plan, you are not starting at zero; you are far ahead of someone with no inkling. It's just as important to build the trail knowledge and physical abilities, as knowledge builds a mature confidence in your ability to get out and back safe and sound and with good—no, wonderful—stories to tell. For something that may be the most rigorous activity attempted in a lifetime, it's best if you are continually in shape, and that means body, mind and especially spirit. You'll want enough energy to sample what life has to offer.

Checklists and timelines leave little to chance and the last minute. Note that my suggested timeline allows six months of preparation. This is a minimum, even if you think you are in shape and prepared. If you are starting from scratch as I did, allow more time to research gear, food, and the facts, tips and techniques of hiking. This timeline hits the highlights for an ambitious hike of a few days or more, but certainly provides guidance for the day trip or a weekender with the children.

I love checklists because with each task completed by a checkmark, you can see a project build to completion. You don't have to wonder what to do next, who should do it and when it should be done, plus you can *see* the end.

As I noted, this milestone checklist is laid out for six months, the minimum time necessary to get yourself, your gear and food, and your trail details together. So begin at the beginning; if, for example, you wish to hike in August, back up six months to February. "Decide where and when to hike," and check off that box for February. Bam! The first milestone is done.

> **THE BRITS AND THEIR DOGS**
> Wherever we went along the England Coast-to-Coast (C2C), there was a dutiful dog. They were herding sheep, splattered with mud, in obvious ecstasy. They were at the B&Bs to greet us with an approving sniff and expectant of having an ear scratched. They were ensconced on laps as if enthroned. And they were in the pubs, usually at the feet of children who were eating a bowl of chips (English french fries, sort of limp, sad creatures with vinegar).
> Or even at the bar. As we entered a pub in Reeth[2], a fella was cozied up to the bar, a hand curled around a pint. At his feet was an enormous Weimaraner, sprawled in perfect repose, as if he knew he belonged there. At the dog's head was an extremely large ashtray half filled with beer! The obvious question uncontrollably leapt from my lips, "Is your dog having a beer?" The cap's answer: "Oh, yah. Me dog loves his pint." You can't make this stuff up!

For planning purposes, fill in tentative dates you wish to complete the rest of the items. That way, you can tentatively have the research on the trailheads done in March, for example. Some find it useful to

---
2 http://www.yorkshire.com/places/yorkshire-dales/reeth

also note the initials of the responsible party. Fill in the remainder of the chart accordingly. Then when you have your periodic meetings, you and your companions have the preparation status at a glance. You will also know who is to do what and when, a most helpful way to goose the tardy along as the hike date looms large. If it is a team effort, you need not nag—the checklist does it for you, which makes meetings much more pleasant too. How about calling a couple of friends and starting one right this minute?

Create a Timeline

HIKER'S TIMELINE OF MILESTONES

EVENT	Month 1	Month 2	Month 3	Month 4	Month 5	Month 6
Decide where and when to hike						
Research or reconnoiter trailheads						
Conduct initial meeting of hikers						
Complete physical exam						
Begin physical conditioning						
Begin better diet						
Reserve accommodations						
Attend classes (if available)						
Procure gear—backpack first						
Train in gear						
Do a short overnight shakedown trip						
Ramp up the physical training						
Procure food						
Procure any prescription medications						
Plan post-trip debrief/critique						
Attend to personal affairs during the trip						
Confirm accommodations and determine trail conditions						
Check weather						
Consider leaving the cell phone behind						
Pack						
Hit the trail						
Conduct post-trip debrief/critique						
Discuss ideas/plan next trip						

CHAPTER 2
Milestones at a Glance

Nature herself makes the wise man rich.
—Cicero

Go wherever your imagination leads you

Now that you've created your timeline in Chapter 1, in this chapter, let's take a closer look at what each of the milestones in the timeline entails. Although we will look at each step in more detail, it's still a cursory glance at this point. We will get into the real nitty-gritty in later chapters.

We will cover each milestone in order, so let's start at the beginning: Where do you want to hike?

Decide Where and When to Hike

There is nothing like starting a project with the end in mind. Pick an experience, any one, preferably one you have always dreamed about. Then, after going through *The Honest Backpacker* so you have an idea of the task ahead, target a time to do so. As always, write a few things about each adventure so you can fairly evaluate each possibility. Begin with your dream trip. Title it with a brief description in a sentence or two, no more. Consider how long the hike is and over what terrain. Also consider the time of year and the weather it may bring. Getting that 35-pound pack up to 7,000 feet and back down a few times on hot, humid days may not be realistic. Although our ultimate goal was the C2C, we discovered that was quite an ambitious feat out of the starting gate, so we decided to do a couple of preparatory hikes as run-ups.

READING AND RESOURCES

There are numerous books, magazines and guides about hiking. Read a few. Even if you are not hiking the Appalachian Trail (AT), check out the AT Conservancy's selections (www.appalachian-trail.org). The AT has been around since early last century, so those folks have a lot of collective wisdom.

From there, get on the internet (see "Resources"). Thereafter, the trick will be what not to read, as it is overwhelming what you can dig up.

Unfortunately, none of it really approaches the topic comprehensively, by considering body, mind and spirit. In addition, the information is usually topic-specific and doesn't consider the comprehensiveness of all the preparation. The biggest problem is that little is directed to the baby boomer, which is why we are documenting what we have learned as boomers, and for boomers.

Research or Reconnoiter Trailheads

Know where you will begin by figuring out how to get on the trail. No matter the hike, you need to know where you will get on and off the trail. Learn where and what the accommodations and campsites are. Set up transportation. Many people have a side business ferrying hikers hither and thither. Or drop off a car at the ending point so you can drive back to the trailhead for the other car. For exceptionally long hikes like the Appalachian Trail (AT), you need to be aware of places where you can go off-trail for a rest to provision and to pick up what the home front has sent ahead—say, a new pair of boots that have already been broken-in. For example, we did our trial run of the AT by getting on at Damascus, Virginia, which put us at a very pleasant 50-mile stretch going south, the opposite way most hikers start, while avoiding rougher hiking at the traditional start point in Springer Mountain, Georgia. We got off the trail in Tennessee and had a local drive us back to Damascus.

Conduct Initial Meeting of Hikers
As soon as possible, gather your fellow hikers. Get to know each other—hiking on an extended trip together is very different from having a beer after work. We had meetings of a few wannabes who disappeared when they got a feel for what was ahead. Ideally, beforehand everyone will have done a little preparation by reading *The Honest Backpacker* or have some hiking experience under their belt. This is when you collectively fill in the timeline and set expectations.

How do you begin anything that is important to the players or even vital because of its potential? If the goals of the endeavor bear repeating, they are to learn and conquer a challenge, make memories and have fun, so make sure your first meeting is well organized, productive and fun, as it sets the stage for what is to come.

First, try to say "backpacking planning party" three times fast. Now, make this the most difficult thing you do while planning. Failing that, plan to meet, eat pizza, talk, dream, set a date and drink beer or wine, which makes for a pretty good planning party agenda anyway. Obviously, the more you can hash out in the beginning, months or a year in advance, the better. Especially if it is the first time for such an expedition, be thorough, but don't get hung up on the process by trying to make it perfect; keep it and you moving. Naturally if your goals are a more modest endeavor, the planning will be a bit shorter.

Do what you can to make your hike a good experience. If planning becomes a drag, do something to lighten the process. Schedule a regular "brewski" to talk about whatever comes up. Maybe do workouts together. Why not do a rotating potluck dinner? There is no limit to what is essentially team building.

As corny as it sounds, it is about the journey and a life well lived. The scope of this book does not lend itself to my elaborating all the unexpected but most welcomed life experiences to which hiking led. Suffice it to say that if you set out to make the process enjoyable, it will be.

MAKE YOUR MEETINGS COUNT

No doubt we all have been to meetings that were simply bad, or worse, a total waste of time. Put some time into meeting planning to make them practical, productive and pleasurable. Here are some ideas to consider:

- **Assign tasks.** There will be much for the group to do, individually and collectively. Review and assign any action items. Give the odd jobs a specific time frame for completion, which makes the preparation process progress despite the procrastinator in the crowd.
- **Field questions.** See if there are outstanding questions from the group and if those questions can be answered internally or referred to outside professionals or other sources.
- **State your purpose.** If folks care to reflect, you may want to ask them to comment on what their purpose or expectation is for doing the hike. This is a good time to bring up any reservations or doubts.
- **Follow up.** Set a subsequent post-trip meeting; it is a great teaching/learning moment and one not to be missed.
- **Wrap up.** End each phase of planning, implementing and doing by reiterating that the result of this preparation and experience is well worth it. Take it in chunks; don't look at the totality of getting ready because over time it is a matter of just filling spare time with things that need to be done by checking them off the to-do list. At worst, you may sacrifice a sitcom or two for an experience of a lifetime. But once done, you can pick up at a moment's notice for any experience in the outdoors. Be ready to do what the trail tells you to do. It may capture you on a bald mountaintop, at a hidden waterfall or in a field of yellow blooms, so linger and enjoy. It is called being flexible, and it is an element of what makes a life worth living.

Begin by filling in the dates in the timeline on page 17 so everyone knows individual responsibilities, even if the hike is just for you and a buddy. Start a contact sheet listing the name, phone, address, email, etc., of your crew so your partner adventurers can converse with each other at will. Appoint or "volunteer" the most tech-savvy of your little band to connect you all via social media. At least, consider creating an email list or Facebook page.

It is remarkable how many topics there are to discuss with a life adventure on the horizon. Start with the ideas and checklists suggested throughout *The Honest Backpacker*; you can always add or delete if necessary. Organize it all in a binder, which can be taken to meetings, or in Google Docs, for example, to allow everyone to comment and build your resources and journal. Those collective edits are the details of future trip planning, well worth the effort because it saves a ton of time on subsequent trips, whether they may be backpacking or not. This is about discovering your path. Remember, the book that suits your every outdoors planning need hasn't been written (except, perhaps, this one).

Complete Physical Exam
It is a good idea to see your health professional, especially if a rigorous experience is planned.

Let your physician know what you are doing. A great time for this is when you have your annual physical. If not, get an appointment, especially if you haven't been to see a doctor in some time. I view a regular visit to my doctor as health maintenance, which is part of a good overall health and fitness regimen. Be sure you discuss any physical fitness plan you anticipate and get an OK to proceed, especially if you plan regular exercise and haven't been too faithful to physical conditioning. *Note:* Walking the dog is activity, *not* exercise.

Begin Physical Conditioning
When the trip is scoped out, it should be obvious how much physical conditioning is needed. Do not take getting in shape for granted. There is nothing so demoralizing as having a lifetime dream dashed because of a sprain or shin splints. Begin slowly but with a resolution to exercise at least three times per week for six months, mainly

to get into the habit of exercising. If you have not exercised for a while, I recommend getting a well-qualified trainer to set you up with some routines matched to your goals and condition and show you how to do them properly to avoid injury. The goal is to work up to honest exercise five times per week for the opportunity to develop well-rounded conditioning that combines flexibility, balance, core, aerobic and anaerobic exercise—in that order of importance. More on this in Chapter 4, "Getting Yourself Ready."

Begin Better Diet
Exercise is good but not half as good without proper nutrition, which considers what lies beyond diet. Let's face it, when it comes to diet, we backslide. I know I cannot say no to a scoop of ice cream, which I justify because I have just eaten a well-proportioned, healthy and balanced meal. Plus, "I'm worth it." So, if you can consult a well-recommended dietitian or nutritionist, that's ideal. I can attest to the fact that a reasonable—meaning not insane—diet combined with sweat-producing exercise five times a week is transformational. I weigh two pounds more than when I was 25, and I am preparing for another triathlon sprint to celebrate a 50-year high school reunion.

Reserve Accommodations
If your goal is a long trail, like the AT, you will need to know where you can stay at the trailhead and at B&Bs along the way. For the AT, we had only to reserve the Lazy Fox Inn in Damascus, Virginia. For the C2C, we had a dozen reservations along the prescribed trail coinciding with the recommended day's hike, which was at its shortest 8 miles and at its longest 22 miles. If you will be roughing it along the way and camping, you should still research and if necessary reserve campsites.

Attend Classes (If Available)
A great way to get as trail smart as possible is to attend classes. Why reinvent the wheel when you can pick the brains of experienced, even expert, outdoors people? With the prospect of selling truckloads of

gear, any outfitter can't wait to get you in their classes. Plus, they are fun. Look into classes offered by REI and other outdoor retailers. A class is a great way to begin buying gear, especially when recommended by experienced outdoor enthusiasts. Pick wisely.

> **TAKE A CLASS**
>
> There are many backpacking classes sponsored by outfitters, outdoors clubs and even your local college. Hit a few of these to begin putting your hike together and develop some comfort with the lingo. Choose classes with hands-on skill building whenever possible. Prepare but don't get paralyzed by endlessly anticipating every possible contingency and detail. When you are reasonably confident, equipped, in shape and have a thorough shakedown trip under your belt, just do it. The trail will teach you, and you can make some minor adjustments along the way. It's all part of the outdoor experience, and there is something neat about getting into the sport by reading, talking and listening to fellow enthusiasts. This is, after all, the road less traveled, even if it's in a national park.

Procure Gear—Backpack First

The backpack is like the foundation to building a house, so this is not the place to go cheap. (Refer to Chapter 7, "Gear," for a shopping list point of departure.) Try it all out in the backyard; putting up a tent correctly and quickly takes practice. And packing a backpack is a bit technical to get right; that, too, will be discussed in Chapter 7. Your goal is to have less than a 30-pound pack, including water. Most new hikers go way over this magic number and end up throwing things away or mailing them back. Hence the need for a shakedown. There is much to figure out. I remember on the first excursion to the Appalachian Trail I did not have my backpack adjusted correctly, and within a few hours of hiking I had worn a hole in my left leg hip flexor, which knocked me off trail to figure it out and rest. While this was fine on the AT, it is not a good idea in the wilds of northern England when one is being attacked by hordes of killer sheep.

Train in Gear

This is nearly too obvious and self-explanatory. Hike a local park in the clothing you will wear on the trail or as close to it as possible. Naturally, if it is winter and you are training for a summer jaunt, dress warmly. The point is you need to put the weighted backpack on, break in your footgear and learn your trekking poles. The backpack can be loaded with first a gallon and then two gallons of water. Carrying a pack is a whole different experience because your center of balance will be different and you will use muscles in new and enlightening ways, so, one more time, *just do it*.

Do a Short Overnight Shakedown Trip

There is much to learn that can only be done on the trail. At least do one shakedown; naturally, if you can, do more until you have reasonable confidence in yourself, your skills and your gear. Equipment, such as your hiking poles, takes some getting used to. Yes, there is a technique to using hiking poles correctly. In fact, done properly, they become extensions of your arms and upper body. Hiking poles, efficiently and correctly used, are mandatory. They involve your arms, shoulders and torso muscles in the work of carrying your load; reassure your feet when going downhill; and even help with stepping out on the straightaway while going through town, the titanium tips clicking the cadence of the road less traveled by. It just takes practice. Setting up a tent is a bit of an art; prepare the ground and place the tent away from any rotten overhead boughs and from the path of rainwater. Learn to set up the stove away from brush just waiting to burst into flames (which I did) and to light the stove, perhaps in the cold, which makes the fuel reluctant to ignite. Learn to attend to a hot spot on a foot with moleskin before it blisters. Well, you get the idea.

> **"Hiking poles, efficiently and correctly used, are mandatory. They involve your arms, shoulders and torso muscles in the work of carrying your load; reassure your feet when going downhill; and even help with stepping out on the straightaway while going through town."**

Ramp Up the Physical Training
With a goal in mind, exercising has purpose, and that purpose helps the "mind over matter" of hitting the gym. A happy circumstance to getting into shape over a matter of months is that it just may become a habit, which is what you want. At this point, you should up the game: Instead of working out three times per week, shoot for the optimal five times per week so you can fit in balance, flexibility, core, aerobic and anaerobic routines. In other words, we're talking yoga, swimming or spinning, some weights, for example, and an age-appropriate CrossFit class or two. Getting in shape is a matter of motivation, and a pending hike does just that.

Procure Food
Naturally, you will want to begin laying out what you will eat. (Refer to Chapter 8, "Food.") Here is where most people go overboard and overweight. You will not starve to death. You will be surprised how frugal you can become with food and still eat well. If you're doing a lengthy trail, like the AT or C2C, by studying your trail, you will most likely find that there are plenty of towns along the way for a quick reprovision. One very experienced hiker we met had a plastic grocery bag slung from a backpack strap, which held a couple of days' worth of gas station food. We don't recommend that, but did I say you meet all kinds?

Procure Any Prescription Medications
Make sure you have any pills and first-aid preparations you may need, prescription or otherwise. With any luck and by being on a healthy diet with exercise, you will need fewer prescriptions and

you will be "trail hardened" to avoid the usual trail maladies, such as blisters, shin splints, and strains or sprains. Some prescriptions require a trip to the doctor, which delays refills. While you are at the doctor's office, let them know what you are doing; they may recommend updating your inoculations and make suggestions for the best ways to soothe common trail ailments, such as stomachaches and foot fungus. Don't forget the vitamins.

Plan Post-Trip Debrief/Critique
While all is aglow immediately after the hike, make sure you review how the whole thing went. It's a great learning experience and entrée to the next hike. Please don't disregard this. It may seem trivial, even anticlimactic, but oh the things you will learn by doing this. It is one thing to celebrate a real accomplishment; it is another to have a great experience and begin planning for the next. You may consider amending your bucket list, as you will dream many a new memory to make.

> **"** While all is aglow immediately after the hike, make sure you review how the whole thing went. It's a great learning experience and entrée to the next hike. **"**

Attend to Personal Affairs During the Trip
It is a bit of an unsettling moment when you are well on your way to the hike or, heaven forbid, on the hike, when you are plagued by the thought that the back door is unlocked. Make a little checklist (I love checklists—did I say that?) to batten down the house, like making sure the water is shut off, the air conditioner is on vacation, the doors are locked, and the garbage is dumped. Hold the mail, pay the bills, and notify the landlord or a neighbor to investigate any suspicious noises or a moving truck loading up all your worldly goods at 2 a.m. You may also want to tell them that you have left on a light that cycles on and off randomly to perhaps deter potential intruders. And let those same people know when you have returned to avoid

them mistaking you for an intruder. Hopefully, they will want to hear about your adventures over something tasty and refreshing; if they don't think of it, suggest it to them. Make it a thank you for watching the home front.

Confirm Accommodations and Determine Trail Conditions

Check those reservations one more time. Better safe than sorry. You can also check local conditions. And if you are staying at a B&B, it is common courtesy to let your hosts know that all is well and you should be seeing them on schedule. While doing so, get a firsthand opinion of trail conditions.

Check Weather

Obvious. Weather is weather; it is best to check it on the day of departure—you know, being forewarned and all that. Conditions on the way or at the trailhead may alter plans slightly, so at least make sure you are prepared. Is it a T-shirt day or a T-shirt and windbreaker one?

Consider Leaving the Cell Phone Behind

As boomers, we may have a communication device or two. Naturally, you may want to take a cell phone, but the battery has a short shelf life. Plus, a cell phone where reception is unreliable is a waste of weight on more than an overnighter. A prepaid phone card is a functional and practical way to cut weight, and there are phones in town, so you can be as connected as you want. If you decide to take your mobile phone, turn it off to conserve the juice, then recharge when taking a trip to town or to spend a well-earned night in a B&B.

Pack

Finally, it's time to get that gear in the backpack. The moment of truth. You are lean, mean, confident and well-outfitted. Pack with confidence, put the pack and poles in the ol' Bentley, have a celebratory adult beverage, and sleep well if you are not too excited. Wake rested, and go with a broad smile.

Hit the Trail

You will come to a point in preparation when you know enough is enough. Are you 100 percent prepared? No. But that's OK. It would be counterproductive to spend most of your time fretting over 10 to 20 percent uncertainty. Any loose ends, barring catastrophe, will be figured out along the way because you have awareness and skills enough to do so.

> **BEING INCOMMUNICADO**
>
> Leave a trip itinerary and map with family or a friend. Spend a little time with them before you depart and explain the map to them. Also, include an estimate of what you expect to do each day of the hike in terms of anticipated mileage and stopping points. Contact them at every opportunity while on the trail to let them know progress or lack thereof. When talking to Mom, keep stories of pain and mutilation to a minimum.

Conduct Post-Trip Debrief/Critique

Again, you owe it to the crew and especially yourself to review how it all went. This is a real learning experience, and when accompanied by food and libation is quite the party. A handy way is to run through the "Hiker's Timeline of Milestones" checklist on page 17 and take notes. This is all to get ready for the next experience and a continuation of the fun while making memories.

Discuss Ideas/Plan Next Trip

Even on a short overnighter, unless you camp in a cave, you are going to meet really great people. The folks who get out and about are a cut above. They are terribly interesting, talented, educated and well-traveled. I make a point of chatting up and even befriending people. They will tell you where to go, in a good way. Talk to one, and you will get at least two fabulous ideas for future trips. Talk to two, and you will have four more ideas, and so on. Jot down what they tell you in your cell phone reminders or your journal; do not leave any tips up to memory. I speak from experience. Check out the ideas when you get back; it takes only a moment. Add them to your debriefing notes, and select the best for your bucket list.

When you are prepared, the actual experience rounds out your education. Really, you become quite competent and experienced rather quickly, as we found out from the hikers who know their way around the cook stove. More than that, you will become a more interesting person—not a bad thing at all.

By now I hope you have moved beyond dreaming of adventure and have decided to do this. Your checklist of milestones on a timeline is personalized and leads to action. There may be a feeling of no turning back, and that is a good thing. Nothing succeeds like action.

Even after you have gone through the timeline and made a commitment to getting out and about, you are becoming more experienced than most at such an undertaking. Furthermore, if you have the experience I did with the process of planning for and then hiking, it will be life changing. Not only will you have memories enough for a nice journal, but you will become a bit healthier, perhaps wiser and certainly more well-rounded. Oh, the friends you will make on this odyssey called hiking, even if that friend is your own grandchild.

> **❝Oh, the friends you will make on this odyssey called hiking, even if that friend is your own grandchild.❞**

The timeline has been executed, and the process transitions from planning to implementation. It's the moment of truth—the time for action. The next section is the process of getting on the trail. But first let's take a trip to England and the Coast-to-Coast hike, more commonly known as the C2C. It's time to tell the tale of the first full day of hiking from St Bees[3] to Ennerdale Bridge.

---

3 http://www.stbees.org.uk/

Ennerdale Water in England's Lake District

STAGE 1: ST BEES TO ENNERDALE BRIDGE

We had to get used to the dead-reckoning, folksy narrative of the guidebook, *Coast to Coast Path: St Bees to Robin Hood's Bay*, by Henry Stedman. "Don't enter forest, but turn left and go through gate, keeping forest and fence to your right." Which gate—this one or that one? What fence—there's no fence! *Oh, that fence!* Note that *every* building is named, including the houses (I need a name for my house).

As usual, upon knocking on the B&B door, we were met by the proprietress, pleasant enough but in retrospect not nearly as nice as what lay ahead. After a much-earned shower and changing out our boots for Crocs, we asked the most important question, "Where is a good pub?" "Fox and Hounds" was the immediate answer, and off we went for an ale and supper.

Along the way we passed one of the dozens of charming local churches we saw along the way, only this one had a vision of a young beauty strolling through the cemetery. We looked and passed a few remarks—all appropriate, of course—and then realized it was Gill (Gillian, who we came to know as we dogged each other on the trail), the young nurse we had met in the B&B in St Bees, who was hiking to think about life. She was getting married soon, and such a trip was a last chance for her to see "my beautiful country" before starting the rigors of being a wife and mother, a career as an emergency room nurse, and life. She had a jaunty pink daypack and no poles, and she could hike the legs off all of us. Anyway, we suggested she join us for dinner. It turned out she was a bit shy to go into the pub on her own; after all, it was not right for a "proper" Englishwoman. She was strolling the nearby churchyard to contemplate a solution to supper and a proper lady's glass of beer (which we were most happy to provide).

The evening was more than charming, with conversation, joking, good ale and good dinners all round. I recall I had some sort of meat pudding in an ale sauce, as it was "most English." I am a bit speechless at Americans who travel to Paris, Bangkok and Buenos Aires and search high and low for a burger and fries. We couldn't pass up dessert, as it was Spotted Dick, a traditional British steamed sponge pudding with currants (the spots). The locals tell us it is named for one of the King Richards, the "Dick" in the Spotted Dick, who loved the stuff. Others say the name of the dessert is derived from "buddick," the Old English word for pudding. Anyway, I was the one who was voted to go to the bartender to put in the dessert order—which is how dinners are ordered in a pub—as my compadres were much too shy to ask for the dessert. He asked me if I wanted ice cream, cream or custard with it. His Scottish accent was so thick that I could not understand the last option, although eventually I did. He kept saying "koostarrrrd, koostarrrrrd," rolling the R's like the good Scotsman he was, hoping with each repetition that this tourist would get the proper English pronunciation. The British are so tolerant and mannerly in the face of ignorance. It was obvious he was asking if I wanted custard with my Spotted Dick.

We ate and chatted till well past 9 p.m., which became the pattern. It is so civilized to eat and converse the evening away. Gill was a constant stream of genuine laughter, and we were charmed out of our boots again. Yes, our Gill was quite a proper Englishwoman! What an emissary for a grand country.

We three intrepid wanderers finally retired to our rooms and then to bed in short order. My tiny room needed the roll-in heater and every inch of the twin comforter. Sleep was good, very good. A slimmed-down English breakfast, vitamins and coffee, and we were off by 9 a.m. Within a half-hour, we faced the utterly magnificent Ennerdale Water. Bilbo Baggins, Frodo, an Elf or an Orc could have come down the trail any moment.

PART II: THE WHOLE PERSON

Wisdom begins in wonder.
—Socrates

The Irish Sea and the beginning of the England Coast-to-Coast
hike along the cliff

Many of us are or should be concerned with the whole person—what it is to be as fit as possible in spirit, mind and body. We are only as strong as our weakest of those three states of being, which combine into the human condition. It is never too late to start. And committing to an experience in nature happens to be as good an excuse as any to begin working on and improving the totality of who we are. In Part II, we will discuss how to get your whole self into shape for your hike. In doing so, the whole becomes greater than the sum of the parts. What you are about to do not only enhances your life, but is life-affirming; you realize over and over again that life is indeed good.

CHAPTER 3
Introduction to the Whole Person

No matter how difficult life gets—with a few exceptions, all of us have or will pass through a few 'valleys of the shadow'—the next day can be the best day of your life. But you have to be vertical for it.
—James Klopovic's philosophy of life

Hikin' buddies: St Bees in the background on the England Coast-to-Coast

I can think of many instances when life is quite remarkable: How about witnessing the birth of a golden and long-awaited grandchild, seeing a beloved child graduate from school as a physician's assistant after a heroic struggle to do so, remaking an old friendship, reconnecting with a lost family member? Many friends are passing on or are suffering mightily, so much so that they are completely distracted from living; their lives are consumed with the next doctor's visit, the next dose of pills, the next operation and the rest of the day recovering from it all. Nearly universally they lament, "I wish I would have taken better care of myself." Oh, it was fun living it up in their 20s, but they would trade it all for a healthier today and certainly a healthier tomorrow. But there's hope.

I also have a dear friend who got the wake-up call of a tough diagnosis akin to a death sentence. He refused the pills and injections and redid his entire diet, quit alcohol, exercised more, and devoted his considerable energies to family, church, business and raising remarkable German Shorthaired Pointer dogs. In his own way, he put body, mind and spirit together, beat a rotten diagnosis, and is proof positive that the whole is greater than the sum of the parts. In so many ways, so is a hike.

What Is "The Whole Person"?

The concept of the whole person is nothing new. The ancients of many cultures philosophized about it, wrote about it and practiced it. In fact, when summarizing a lifetime of study, the Japanese samurai and teacher Miyamoto Musashi simply stated in Principle 9: *Do nothing which is of no use*[4]. Even leisure can be useful, according to the ancient Romans. Hiking and communing with nature, when approached with some determination and discipline, is a way to reinvent one's self. Enhancing this trilogy of the human condition is synergistic and continuous. It is synergistic because one element can't be isolated from the next. As one grows or deteriorates, so do the others. It is continuous because one simple change only brings us to another vantage point from which to view how we can further enhance our being.

Reaching our full potential is tough. Few mechanisms for self-improvement are as adept at the task as taking a hike. Well, enough philosophy. Let's introduce each element of the trilogy. We begin by considering our physical condition, as for most of us, taking care of the temple seems most problematic.

Body: Establish a Physical Fitness Regimen

There is much to do to get your body in shape (see Chapter 4, "Getting Yourself Ready"). Don't take the easy route. Face the fact

---

[4] *The Book of Five Rings* by Miyamoto Musashi. This book takes many readings and regular refreshers to digest. While the author writes in martial terms, it is an analysis of the human condition and a guide to living. It is one of the more significant books ever written, and a copy was found in Napoleon's mobile command post at Waterloo.

that exercise is work. Immediately establish an exercise routine for flexibility, core (including balance), aerobic and anaerobic (upper body and lower body), *in that order.* Then do a pack-on (loaded pack) hiking simulation. And don't forget diet: Physical fitness is a marginal occupation without the proper nutrition. What better time to contemplate eating a bit more healthfully and perhaps taking a few judiciously chosen vitamins (though the research is now showing that a good diet alone is much better)? You cannot wait to get in shape on the trail. Backpacking is harder than you might imagine, especially if you are not fit.

> **"Reaching our full potential is tough. Few mechanisms for self-improvement are as adept at the task as taking a hike."**

Develop a comfortable level of technical expertise as part of the physicality of preparation. That means know your equipment and how to hike and orient yourself. Plan and prepare enough to feel comfortable in your trail worthiness when things go wrong. Yes, *when*, not *if*; it is inevitable. You will get bug bites. You will become hot, quite hot, in the summer. In the winter, you will get cold. You will look for water. You will get wet, probably very wet. Something will ache. Preparation keeps little snags just that: little. The idea is to keep trail problems limited to those that will make for glorified stories of your prowess in the wilderness, rather than examples for search and rescue teams to use in training scenarios.

Mind: Investigate Mindfulness

Learning to be still while clearing the mind of the confusion of thoughts that constantly swirl around chaotically helps us cope with stress and prolongs life. It also helps us pause throughout the day to contemplate better choices, no matter what they are. The benefits of practicing mindfulness for about a half-hour per day are research-based (a quick internet search will reveal a wealth of studies supporting it). Mindfulness is simply being aware and present in the moment. The practice of clearing one's mind from distractions and acknowledging bodily sensations is therapeutic. What can one expect with practice? While I still have far to go, for me it is an enhanced awareness and attempted dismissal of inconsequential "small stuff" that distracts from my appreciation of and work on what is important: living with as few regrets as possible.

Spirit: Getting "Up" for the Trip
Becoming excited about your trip is important. It's a lot of work, but keep focused on the fact that this may very well be a life accomplishment, in that you are improving your lifestyle and consequently enhancing your quality of life. Preparation leads to confidence that you can handle the physical and technical demands of being self-sufficient without TV and texting. Again, the goal is to be able to look past the exertion of a strenuous undertaking to further trips. Boomers who make it to retirement can expect to be vigorous into their 90s; that gives us time for yet another career, getting *it* right, or, as Ben Franklin did, "correct errata." (See Chapter 10, "Correcting Errata.") Just have reasonable expectations of yourself and your trip.

Set Realistic Expectations
First and foremost, we must consider diet in the same breath with which we talk about the physical preparation for getting outside and beyond the evening news, which seamlessly oozes into "must-see TV"—and, poof, the evening is shot. Diet will probably be the major occupation of your physical preparation, since eating is frequent and may (will) require adjustment. We are well advised to unlearn bad habits that we may have come by the hard way. It took us years to get comfortable with the way we eat, and more than likely, it is not what we need or what we can be proud of. If you are the usual boomer wanting to make amends at the table, it is a struggle. We would go so far as to say that the correct diet is at least, and probably more than, 70 percent of the battle of getting off the couch and onto the trail. Again, this *is* the road less traveled—and worth it. If you need a life-changing event, take a hike!

Introduction to the Whole Person

> **"** Boomers who make it to retirement can expect to be vigorous into their 90s; that gives us time for yet another career, getting it right, or, as Ben Franklin did, 'correct errata.' **"**

You must be in shape enough to get in shape to attempt hiking. It is tough, even counterproductive, to stay in peak condition all the time. We are not pro or elite athletes. What I mean is that you should have a goal to be continuously fit just enough to ramp up your conditioning for a specific event and peak just before it. So use your adventure as the best of reasons to become better physically, enough to be continuously ready for anything you wish to do. This philosophy of maintaining health also keeps you better fit mentally and spiritually while minimizing the chances of injury or being defeated by the prospect of getting in shape for another life experience from a near-zero condition. After all, you can't have flown a desk for years and expect a miracle. As with any task, if broken down into essential elements they become much easier to tackle; the same applies to exercise.

It's All in Your Mind

The idea of any pursuit, such as this hiking business, is to manage the inevitable glide-slope of aging. The neat thing about all this is that once you are into it, you will find there are all sorts of opportunities for honest-to-goodness exercise, and you will want to do more than the five hours per week for health purposes. Join any gym, for example, and you will be connected to perhaps a chain, and each one of them has dozens of guided exercise classes, most of which combine all exercise groups (core, balance, flexibility, aerobic and anaerobic). When you are surrounded by people who are concerned about general health—fitness and mental—and well-being, you can be drawn into many other activities, if you so choose. I got exposed to skiing, skydiving, snorkeling, SCUBA, road biking and a few more things I can't recall. One activity begets another; it is simply a neat state of moving in the right direction.

Consider the mindful aspect. You become more mindful when

preparing for an outdoor experience. You may even want to study up on mindfulness, as we discussed above. Many brand-name medical schools—Duke and Harvard, for example—include mindfulness as part of the training for and practice of medicine. There is something to be said about learning to meditate, which you can do with any of life's occupations, like walking, eating or shooting skeet. Yes, shooting skeet, as clearing the mind and developing complete relaxation is *the* key to making an effective shot repeatedly!

You should be prepared with enough study, contemplation, research and perhaps taking a few notes on the side to build a body of knowledge that encompasses your outdoors undertaking and that will keep you safe, secure and moving on the trail. Again, you will want to do this preparation as time progresses and the hike gets closer.

While you are getting in physical shape, all your bodily functions work better, whether it is thinking, sleeping or digesting. One of the surprising things to me is that even a senior citizen can put on muscle with a good exercise program. The trick is to plow through the drudgery until it becomes part of a new lifestyle.

CHAPTER 4
Getting Yourself Ready: Physical Fitness

He is richest who is contented, for content is the wealth of nature.
— William de Britaine

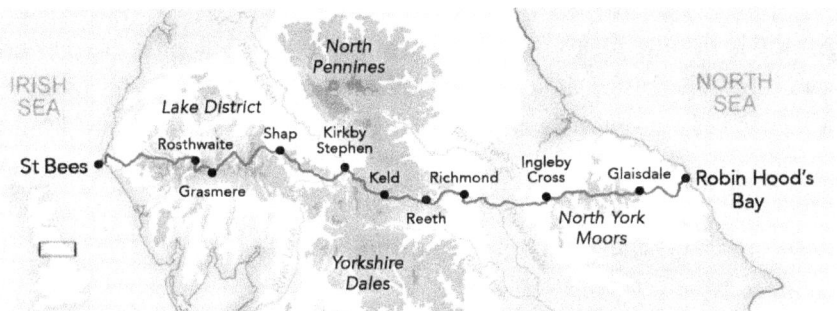

The suggested stops along the 192 miles of the England Coast-to-Coast hike

Let's face it, the mature hiker is different from the 20-something, and for that matter the 30- and in many cases the 40-something. It is harder to get out of the sack in the morning, and recovering from a workout or an injury takes forever. I'm sure you know that. But pause and make a note here, before we begin our discussion of the actual training. Bob Peoples, owner and proprietor of Kincora Lodge (see "Acknowledgements"), had an observation about getting on the trail: "If you have a mind to get in the woods, just get out there." This message must be taken to heart. While we suggest throughout these pages that you are well advised to do quite a bit of planning, preparation and even more to get the older boomer physically, psychologically and mentally ready, there are lots of folks who just blast off for a day or two and have a great time. It doesn't matter how you are introduced to the outdoors; what matters is that you get out there. Naturally, a longer, more physically demanding endeavor will take more forethought and preparation.

Enjoying the outdoors is infectious. The more you put into it, the more you get out of it—isn't that life? Bob's counsel also implies that getting out and about adds more zest, purpose, and a dash of the exciting, enticing and unknown about the next day, and the next and the next. You learn so much, especially in unexpected moments. There is nothing like being exhausted and lying back on nature's own bedding and instantly finding it is stinging nettles. Luckily, I was only witness to this teachable moment.

Further, and this is as important as any advice for the older hiker, hiking is *not* meant to be all-consuming. It is only a part of a varied and interesting life. Make time also for mindfulness classes, growing a tomato plant on the patio, having a beer with a dear friend, and going to the movies and holding hands with the love of your life. Be endlessly entertained while entertaining children, especially grandchildren. With these thoughts in mind, let's continue.

> "Hiking is *not* meant to be all-consuming.
> It is only a part of a varied and interesting life."

Let's address getting the body ready. This is our first topic in the trilogy that is the human condition, followed by the mind and the spirit (meaning the zest we can have for life). Without the body, it is tough to get the mind and spirit doing very much. You *must* get your physical self ready. An injury or undue discomfort will turn you off to the whole experience quite prematurely. Physical preparation is not something you approach lightly, nor need it be something akin to being chained to an oar on a Roman war galleon, where the beatings continue until morale improves. Approach it with seriousness and an intent to have fun at the same time. But do give exercising a good go. Do it long enough that your exercise routine becomes habitual. Work up to exercising five days per week, and do it for at least six months, as that is the time required to build this kind of habit.

The first thing in preparing physically is to make sure the diet is healthy while providing the nutrition and fuel needed for the correct, meaning age appropriate, increased activity.

Discipline, Diet and Common Sense

Don't even contemplate getting in shape unless you put diet and nutrition first. Even if you are somewhat fit, use this experience to evaluate and adjust your dietary habits. Diet is more than half the battle, but once you conquer the dark side of fast-food temptation and bad eating and drinking habits, you are left with a very tolerable, if not pleasant, dietary lifestyle. Think of this as a lifelong nutritional regimen, not just one you will follow for a few weeks after the new year.

To be a successful hiker, you need a knowledge of nutrition to keep yourself well-fueled for vigorous, extended activity. And the proper fuel is a whole lot different from the morning rush you get from the pervasive "Pop-Tart" diet.

Three Simple Rules

Diet is discipline and common sense; a few simple rules will help you stick with your newly adopted healthy eating habits. However, simple does not mean easy. Try not to fall into the trap of fad dieting. Do not succumb to the latest ab-cruncher infomercial that promises godlike results "in only 20 minutes per day, three days a week." It is amazing that kind of hucksterism abounds. But I digress.

Pick a diet program that seems reasonable. Before starting any diet, consult with a medical professional and check in regularly as well.

To build the habits of a meaningful, productive lifestyle means being disciplined for six to 12 months. No matter what Madison Avenue says, it takes that kind of commitment to change a lifetime of mind-altering by advertising, convenience and flashing neon lights.

Living a healthy lifestyle means following these three simple rules:
1. *No refined sugar*: The bad news is this eliminates most of what we eat, or at least most of the choices we have thrust upon us from every direction, every waking hour.
2. *No refined flour*: Guess what? This rule and the one above eliminate Krispy Kremes. Actually, they apply to all three rules. Sorry. Don't worry, though, this is going in a good direction.
3. *No trans/hydrogenated fats*: Which all but eliminates processed and fast foods.

Many health professionals would also add eliminating extra salt. There is plenty that occurs naturally in a balanced diet.

The bad news is these rules cut out nearly 110 percent of the food we typically see daily. The good news is, there are plenty of better alternatives that, when given a chance, the body craves. The natural fructose found in fruits and veggies can sub for sugar; whole flours, especially sprouted grain breads, are very acceptable; and the Italians have been doing quite well on olive oil instead of butter for a few millennia. Some nutritionists suggest coconut oil is a good substitute for bacon fat. Let sensibility rule your dietary choices. Many cultures are known for high-calorie diets—take the French, for example—but they practice portion control.

Most of us struggle with diet; only a few do not. But a healthy diet is doable and becomes part of an overall campaign to get ready for the back country, even if it is the local park. Think of it as a clever way of disguising something you wanted to do anyway. And just think: When you make progress, most folks will be pleasantly surprised at the results, and the remainder will be astounded. Attitude is paramount.

Diet Attitude

These suggestions are just the beginning of the road to staying healthy. Health is also a lifestyle, part and parcel of a wholesome body, mind and spirit. Any suggestions made about diet are meant to be common sense and done in concert with the whole-person concept. Good diet works only with regular exercise, as prescribed in *The Honest Backpacker.*

Be smart, sensible and determined. Diet means discipline seven days a week. It means routine. Don't skip a meal to make up for the cookie you just had to have. Soon, you won't miss the cookie. Being sensible, though, can also mean a forgivable but modest splurge on a good, balanced, home-cooked meal or a birthday dinner at a fine restaurant with modest portions, including the dessert. Occasional splurges are good for the soul, and that is also *vital* to good nutrition. Many healthy people have a modest percentage of blood comprised of good Bordeaux and butter. The body and especially the mind will *not* follow a discontented soul.

However, there is a limit to splurging. Diet and exercise also mean *no* harmful substance abuse, legal or illegal. End of discussion. End of paragraph.

> **"**Many healthy people have a modest percentage of blood comprised of good Bordeaux and butter. The body and especially the mind will *not* follow a discontented soul.**"**

A healthy lifestyle also means avoiding foolish behavior; safety, for example, should become second nature. "Eat not to dullness; drink not to elevation" (as Benjmain Franklin advised); don't smoke; and don't run with scissors. As stated previously, don't fall into unsafe fad diets and exercise. You don't need to look like a magazine cover model or "feel the burn" so much that you constantly damage muscles and joints by going at it unreasonably hard. A current fad is the Insanity workout; it is just that, insanity. It is an accident waiting to happen, especially for a boomer, and so tough as to discourage the pursuit of exercise altogether.

A better idea is to be conservative enough in your activity that you can keep fit and toned without dreading exercise or killing yourself. What matters is doing a variety of honest exercise that breaks a good sweat. Physically fit can be as simple as getting to the top of a flight of stairs and not be out of breath. I personally like the stated purpose of a rigorous, yet age-appropriate, CrossFit class—that is, to be able to carry a bag of dog food.

Being *in* shape has nothing to do with an idealized shape. A pear is a shape, too; even a pear can be fit. There are a million examples. Take Julia Child. She never shied away from the sauce, whether in the glass or over French vanilla ice cream, but it was in moderation and with great sensibility. Throw in the fact that she pursued her passion while staying active, and you have a role model for how to grow old, vigorous, graceful and productive well into your 90s.

There is another element to realism: Don't expect much from *any* fitness scheme initially. Rest assured, there will come a day when you will be pleasantly surprised, but in small ways. That, again, is what it is all about. Do this because it is the right thing to do.

> **"**Being *in* shape has nothing to do with an idealized shape. A pear is a shape, too; even a pear can be fit. There are a million examples. Take Julia Child. She never shied away from the sauce, whether in the glass or over French vanilla ice cream, but it was in moderation and with great sensibility.**"**

You may hope to shed a few pounds, but don't expect *anything* if you deviate from the plan. It is too easy to cascade back to old habits. You are establishing new habits, and that takes a reasonable amount of time and discipline. This does not mean you must live the life of a monk. When you are satisfied with the progress you have made and your healthy lifestyle is permanent, then go ahead and indulge on a Sunday; just don't go overboard. Remember to continually monitor your weight and vital statistics, such as blood pressure, cholesterol and heart rate. But during this time of restructuring habits, it means you are not permitted a cookie crumb, a lick of the batter spoon or a sample of ice cream. Of course, once a good diet regimen is established, it's quite OK to enjoy a meal of your favorites once a week—just control the portions. Slow down; be mindful of every bite.[5] A little splurge is good for the soul. But be cautious; it is a slippery slope.

Remember, you are recreating, relearning and redirecting a lifestyle that may be the result of decades of bad habits. It also means not one or two days at the gym, but at least three days per week where you work hard on cardio and core and the other two days on flexibility and weights.

---

[5] If you get into mindfulness, you may learn to eat mindfully, which means eating very slowly while you savor all the sensations—taste, feel, smell, and it's art on the plate—of what you are eating. Mindful eating also helps you eat less.

It also means your path is just that, yours. Put together a program, and do it. Read, study, do it, experience it, alter it to adjust to your changing needs and perspective. Just spend some honest time every day devoted to the body, mind and spirit. Remember, no one else is responsible for what goes into your mouth, or how many reps you do and when, or what you read and think.

Pause for a moment and think about what all this means to you and where it might take you. Be quixotic. I think about a cooking vacation hosted by the matron of the family at a 500-year-old wine estate overlooking the coast of Sicily and helping with the grape harvest: imagine the food, camaraderie, sweat, good wine, new friends, song, dance, stories, laughter and fantastic memories.

Now let's consider age, which is twofold: your chronological age, which is the number of years you have been alive, and your real age, which is a composite of all the factors of living good and not so good.

BE AWARE OF YOUR REAL AGE

There are myriad factors that comprise health. One of the best books for an explanation of more than 100 of these factors can be found in *RealAge: Are You as Young as You Can Be?* by Michael Roizen, M.D. Most everyone is, in fact, older or younger than their chronological age, depending on heredity, habits and how they get through the day. Most of the book is common sense and written for the layperson. Its value is in cueing the reader to make minor adjustments to living that collectively make a large difference. For example, you will probably choose to take a few select vitamins and minerals, even though research is determining that vitamins have marginal effects.[6] However, it's not a good idea to take supplements, especially as a meal replacement. Just look at all the ingredients in these products. Some simple words of wisdom serve as general guides:

- **Eat what grows in the earth, not what walks on it.** Well, OK, a little lean chicken, fish (not fish sticks or fried), and the occasional lean pork chop. And please excuse me for having sweet potato fries seasoned with cinnamon, a range-fed beef burger with sautéed mushrooms on a Kaiser roll, and a pint of

---

6   http://www.webmd.com/vitamins-and-supplements/news/20131216 experts-dont-waste-your-money-on-multivitamins

Belgian ale at the Copper Penny in Wilmington, North Carolina, to celebrate doing that triathlon sprint. Hey, life is *good*.

- **Eat around the edges of a grocery store, not from what is in the aisles.** If you do that, you will hit the veggies and less processed foods.
- **Look at ingredient panels.** The first ingredients comprise the bulk of the item. See how many begin with some sort of refined sugar in the top three and progress to the unpronounceable. And if you can't pronounce them, they are usually not good for you.

Additionally, the medical community and nutritionists assure us that all we need comes from eating a balanced diet of the correct foods. In the final analysis, supplements don't work well, especially when they are substitutes for a balanced diet of good foods.

I find it helpful to bag up my current regimen of vitamins, which gets smaller every few years or so, and take them to my annual physical, where my doctor of the past 30 years can pass judgment. He has them down to half of what they were, and the remainder are only taken by choice. At least take that children's aspirin every evening, which over time appears to be a wonder drug. Just know the pros and cons, which can be found with a quick Google search. There is no effort, the expense is minimal, and, hey, it doesn't hurt. For example, I fought a left hamstring pull for years. It was uncomfortable to exercise, and I thought I would carry it to my grave. I realized it was gone after a few weeks of including a dose of glucosamine with the multivitamin I had been taking for a few years and still do. Coincidence? Perhaps, but who's to say?

I was further pleasantly surprised by studying the book *RealAge* that being healthy also means wearing your seatbelt, never exceeding the speed limit by more than 5 mph, not riding a motorcycle (organ delivery mechanism), and not skydiving (only once). It was a gestalt moment to learn that being fit is not merely diet and exercise, but simply being logical. A large hunk of being fit requires absolutely no perspiration at all, just a little research, consultation, forethought and application of your brain.

DO YOU REALLY NEED THAT STATIN?

My personal physician summarily announced after the bloodwork for my annual physical that he was going to put me on a statin. He said it would reduce my risk of a cardiovascular event by 25 percent. "Hold the phone," I said. "Tell me more." He explained that they now monitor cholesterol, blood pressure and age to assess health. "Well, what is my risk of those three factors?" I probed. "Twelve percent," he triumphantly announced. So, I would risk all the significant downsides of a statin to reduce my risk by a mere 3 percent. But when you're talking heart attacks, even 3 percent may be too much risk. Some quick research determined that I had low HDL (the good stuff), but not very high LDL (the bad stuff), which is what the statin would attack, still leaving HDL as the problem. In other words, I would still have a cholesterol problem, even *with* the statin.

I checked further and found that there is a test for blood calcium, which is a measure of the viscosity of the blood, hence the propensity to have cholesterol stick to the arteries. If it is low, good. I had the test, and it was really low—a miniscule .4 of the maximum of 10, to be exact—due to a reasonably healthy lifestyle. Furthermore, the biggest risk factor of the three is age, and I can't do anything about that. In fact, I encourage getting older. So, the punch line is, with a good lifestyle, which we have been talking about, I can avoid, if not eliminate, a course of medicine that has real side effects of muscle aches, possible liver damage and a decrease in mental functioning (on top of going into a room and forgetting why I went there)—and that is only what they know so far. I remain off the statin and hope to continue so.

Another important thing to internalize is that we are not meant to last forever. Furthermore, it is not a good idea to try to beat aging; it is going to happen. It is genuinely *good* to grow old, hopefully with a few marbles, some grace and some capability left.[7] But we should do what we can to face what is arguably the best years of our lives with as much energy, ability, enthusiasm, realism and humility as dictated by our God-given lot. In the final analysis, or at least at the end of the day, you are your own best physician.

---

[7] I recommend reading *Cicero: Selected Works, Part Two: How to Live*, Chapter 5; "Cato the Elder on Old Age."

> **"It is genuinely good to grow old, hopefully with a few marbles, some grace and some capability left."**

So, to begin getting yourself physically in better shape, decide on a reasonable diet, one perhaps recommended by a health care professional, and stick to it.

The 40-30-30 Plan

There is so much ado about diet that it almost doesn't warrant mention. There is no trick to eating healthy; you either do it or don't. Again, what matters is that you do something sensible. More than likely, it will be a combination of eating smarter and less of what has been getting past your lips for too many years, whether you need to lose a pound or two. We just don't need the calories to which we have access. My dear grandmother admonished in her heavy Croatian accent, "Don't eat with your eyes." Somehow that applies now as much as ever. We are descendants of prehistoric man who subsisted on leafy things, seeds, fruits, nuts, roots and an occasional unlucky rabbit. Besides, everyone then walked a lot to get those prehistoric subsistence calories. Backpacking returns us to our evolutionary roots.

> **"My dear grandmother admonished in her heavy Croatian accent, 'Don't eat with your eyes.' Somehow that applies now as much as ever."**

So a good point of departure is the book *The Formula: A Personalized 40-30-30 Weight Loss Program*, by Gene and Joyce Daoust. Much of it is an advertisement for rather expensive supplements. (If you decide to take any supplements, research them well. Many high-end trainers recommend natural foods to get and stay in shape.) The wisdom of the piece is in the fact that the healthy organism needs about 40 percent carbohydrates, 30 percent proteins *and* 30 percent fats, but the proper kind and in the correct proportion of

Getting Yourself Ready: Physical Fitness

each, kind of like a caveman may have had, though I am not recommending the Caveman diet, which is another fad.

While the title suggests that everyone needs to lose weight, the suggested regimen and types of foods make some sense, especially for maintenance. Further, it suggests a day of rest, the seventh day of dieting, when you can cheat a little bit with some of the (proper and balanced) foods you love (note that the emphasis is on the "little bit"). When one has been on this or any proven diet for even a little while, there is the realization that weight can be managed and that the task is sensible, if not logical. The logic is that the human organism probably evolved with a diet of roughly the proportions of the three main essential nutritional groups specified in the title of the Daoust book. We are simply returning to eating what is natural. In fact, the body craves the natural balance of nutrition and exercise if given the chance.

In truth, it is tough to make this the model for eating for the rest of your life. It's Spartan. Goodness knows, life is short and one needs the occasional steak, tater with sour cream and a little scoop of custard-based vanilla ice cream right from the mixer. If not, you are in danger of irreversible brain damage and perhaps insanity. Moderation is always the key. For example, I find it is quite easy to cook a half cup of oatmeal with hemp seeds, fruit and almond milk nearly every morning, and that is all you need for breakfast. Well, a good cup of coffee must be included also. Let your body tell you what it needs. By referring to a table of your daily caloric requirements in the attachments of the *40-30-30* book, you can monitor exercise, diet and overall bodily functions to make sure it augments your pursuit of better health, rather than detracts from it.

The extent of my technical monitoring of fitness and weight is my belt. If it seems to be getting snug, I just tighten the diet/exercise discipline a bit. After all, it is much easier to maintain a good weight and fitness level rather than must claw back from being overweight and out of shape. By the way, I have been on the same belt setting since my mid-20s; this is just stating the fact that this way of living works.

We were amazed on the trail at how little food one needs, and we were burning 4,500 calories on a day of hiking, at least when one figures a hiking hour requires about 500 calories, give or take. Furthermore, once you are in better shape, especially if that condition has been proved on a goodly hike, there need be no guilt about the occasional sensible indulgence at the table. But you need to get there from here.

Keeping with the intent of this book not to repeat too much that can be retrieved from a publication or from the internet, it may still be helpful to review a suggested daily schedule of meals, which are recommended in the *40-30-30* book. You can get what you need from cursory research or even, heaven forbid, the old-fashioned way at the library. I found that it was not difficult to stay on the diet, although it got a little repetitive, mainly due to the lack of creativity on my part. Note also the frequency of meals. It is sensible to eat five times per day, which personal trainers recommend when you are in training or trying to tone up, but in smaller, more balanced amounts, with the emphasis on fruits, veggies and lean proteins, kind of like the human species evolved. There are so many ways to approach what and how you eat. Just do what is manageable, sensible and relatively easy to accommodate, since you want eating well and healthy to become a habit. So, a point of departure is in order.

Getting Through the Day: A Daily Schedule of Meals

It is unfair to pass judgment on what it is like to change your nutritional intake. It most likely will take some getting used to if you are used to breakfast in a can or plastic wrap. After going through such a regimen and once you get past the initial and normal mind-over-matter phase, you settle into better meals. You will find that you most likely won't be hungry, as meals are necessarily quite frequent to match the increase in activity. Remember, this is just an example. When you get into it, there are entire books devoted to pleasing the palate while cutting calories and cholesterol (the bad LDL kind; conversely, diet is also the best way to increase the good cholesterol, HDL).

I suspect you are getting the picture by now. It is the road less traveled, or, better yet, finding a fork in the road and taking it (aren't life observations from Yogi Berra the best?).

- **Meal 1**: *Breakfast*: 3 egg-white omelet, 1 whole-grain pancake, 1 slice whole-grain toast, 1 piece of fresh fruit
- **Meal 2**: *Mid-morning snack*: 1 piece of fresh fruit, 2 slices of whole-grain bread, 1 chicken breast, 6 oz. skim milk
- **Meal 3**: *Lunch*: 1 half grapefruit, 1 broiled chicken breast, 1 apple, 1 cup kidney beans, 8 oz. skim milk
- **Meal 4**: *Supper*: 8 oz. fruit juice, 1 broiled chicken breast, 1 medium vegetable salad, 6 oz. skim milk
- **Meal 5**: *Mid-evening snack*: Well before bed, preferably before 8 p.m., have 3 egg whites scrambled, 1 small vegetable salad and one slice of whole-grain bread.

Just one more note on the daily meals above from the Daousts' 40-30-30 weight-loss book: I purposely did not mention the calories for each meal and for the day. Caloric intake is a very individual thing driven by age, gender, activity level and purpose. What is more important is learning what good foods and appropriate calories are all about and how to get them. There is a difference between a fruit smoothie and a malted milkshake, even though the calories may be similar.

Moreover, no diet should suggest you give up completely on taste. No high-calorie condiments can be used. Spray canola or coconut oils may be used to make the omelets, which can be flavored with a *little* salt and pepper or salsa. And salads can take a tablespoon or so of vinegar and oil. Our suggestion is to hold fast to reasonable eating for 21 days. Usually, if you have been keeping faithful to common-sense living, exercising regularly and this suggested pattern of eating, there will be results, even if the results are a slightly looser belt and not being as dizzy at the top of a flight of stairs; give it time.

It goes without saying: You need to prepare yourself and your surroundings for these changes. Rid the house of any temptations. That includes the bag of Doritos you have stashed in the shoebox in the back of the clothes closet and the chocolate in the plastic bag in the toilet tank. Let folks know what you are about. Keep records of what you eat, especially if it is *not* on the plan you have for yourself.

And know 21 days is not that long. Set small goals, like seeing your big toes for the first time. And most important, get ready for it . . . if you set out to have fun, you will.

You have your mind right, and the diet is firmly in place. Also, your confidence about your capability to do all this should be building, the adventure is underway, and I dare say, you may be having fun along the way. Now let's get a little exercise going.

Getting In Shape for Boomers

One quick and dramatic comment: *The primary object of exercise for the boomer is* not *to get injured!*

When considering exercise, especially if it has been years since any real, sustained, vigorous activity, the phrase to follow is: *slow as she goes*. The goal is to avoid injury that stops your exercise regimen, and the trick is to learn enough about your physical structure and capabilities that you can continue your regimen by working around an injury, within reason and sensibility. Rest if you must, just make sure that rest is not permanent. There is always something you can do to sweat for an hour. If you pull a muscle in an arm, do lower-body exercises and aerobics until you can resume work with that muscle group. Remember: When recovering, always ease back into things.

> **❝** The primary object of exercise for the boomer is *not* to get injured! **❞**

What Kind of Exercise Are We Talking About?

Physically your regimen needs to consider aerobic and anaerobic exercise; upper-body and lower-body routines; strength and endurance; and most important for my older readers, balance, flexibility and core strength. In fact, aging folks would be well-advised to reverse the above priority of exercising we may have learned in our 20s. So, at the top of the list for exercising is flexibility, core and balance, then comes aerobic and anaerobic exercises. Furthermore, each area for exercise is altered to respect our age. The best thing for flexibility is yoga; it is also good for core and especially balance.

A strong core is the best preventive medicine or palliative for a bad back. The best time to do any exercise is after a good warm-up, so doing core after, say, a spin on the stationary bike is ideal (about 15 minutes of core after a 45-minute spin, for example, will do it). If you do yoga regularly, many times it can supplant physical therapy and drugs.

Aerobic exercises need to be no- or low-impact to preserve what is left of our ankles, knees, hips and backs. So running on hard surfaces for very long distances is out. That dictates spin classes, swimming, a rowing machine, or a medium-speed treadmill jog while mastering the triathlon shuffle, which means keeping the feet as parallel to the jogging surface as possible to minimize the impact of bouncing up and down.

Anaerobic exercises are the reverse of what we may have done in our younger days. Instead of doing big weights with a few reps, it is much better to do low weights, high reps, and timed sets with only a break of 30 seconds between sets. This also builds endurance as it approaches the benefits of scientifically proven high intensity interval training (HIIT). HIIT focuses on a series of intense exertions for about 20 seconds, rest for 10 seconds and then repeated eight times. It is done very nicely on a spin bike. The same can be done with resistance training: light weights, high repetitions. I have also found that a well-supervised CrossFit class is simply great for all-around fitness. Again, this is not the Ninja stuff on TV, which is ridiculous for the boomer. The idea of all this is to increase endurance and maintain strength by toning the body and gradually arriving at an optimal body weight and condition, which you will note by your increased general vigor.

I repeat, any exercise regimen and any class must honor the needs and abilities of everyone. When a new instructor shows up for a class, I find it most helpful to take them aside to let them know my priorities and abilities for their class. Number 1 is to avoid injury, and number 2 is to promote general fitness and well-being. If the instructor does not demonstrate they get me, I modify the routine or dump the instructor.

Approaching fitness via core, balance, flexibility, aerobic and anaerobic routines provides a genuine opportunity for a dizzying array and variety of exercises and activities into which to dive literally and figuratively. There is no time to be bored. There are many apps (Fitness Buddy, for example) that suggest hundreds of exercises and dozens of sequences. Throughout the week, you can devote a lunch hour or an hour before or after work; just do it long enough that you develop the habit of going somewhere to exercise. There are few people who can honestly work out at home, as there are too many distractions and disruptive life patterns. Perhaps you can schedule weights and flexibility three times per week. Core and aerobic exercises on alternate days, perhaps three times per week. My routine is to exercise at noon, a habit of a lifetime of exercising during the lunch hour. Monday is CrossFit. Tuesday is swim; a good goal is a mile eventually. Wednesday is spin and yoga. Thursday is yoga, and Friday is CrossFit. Notice that core, flexibility and balance (yoga) are done twice per week. Aerobic exercise (swim and spin) is done two times also. And CrossFit covers the anaerobic front twice. Also, try to do something active on the weekend, preferably with friends and especially family.

Generally, try to vary things to keep the boredom factor as low as possible. The rule is to vary an anaerobic routine every six weeks to "shock" the muscles into strengthening. That's why CrossFit works so well. Supervised routines change with *every* workout. It is tough work. So, any way you can motivate yourself, whether by signing up for classes, setting goals, monitoring your progress, or having set times and places to exercise, do it.

> **"Approaching fitness via core, balance, flexibility, aerobic and anaerobic routines provides a genuine opportunity for a dizzying array and variety of exercises and activities into which to dive literally and figuratively. There is no time to be bored."**

As the hiking date approaches, there are mock hikes on the treadmill or stair stepper with and without a full pack, with varied speeds and inclines. Among all that, you can throw in a little skeet shooting, biking, a fishing trip or a game of racquetball. All this routine is meant to form positive habits, open opportunities, learn new things and meet new people. Let me say it in another way: If you are not having fun, do something else. If it is not natural, like an intense Ninja workout, don't do it; it even sounds a bit crazy. Fun here also means the sense of accomplishment of getting into better shape.

Make Exercise a Habit
The hard part is simply starting to exercise again, then getting to the gym daily. You will probably find that if you manage to make it to the gym where you have some workout buddies and take regular classes, you will find a groove. Oh yes, there are multitudes of excuses not to go. A big one is "I get enough exercise with my gardening and carpentry." No, that is activity; exercise is different as it tests your limits, especially aerobic and anaerobic, and focuses on your overall fitness for life. Approach it like a religion. They say that 90 percent of success in life is just showing up—and this is so true. But once there, you do have to work.

Again, the idea is to genuinely sweat for an hour of exercise at least five days per week until no excuse gets in the way. You will find every excuse dreamed up by mankind not to get sweaty, when all it takes is to not watch a sitcom or two to have the time to make some important changes. Think about it.

Once you get to the gym or on the treadmill or in the pool, momentum takes over. One day you turn around and your pants are getting a little looser and you don't huff and puff so much at the top of the stairs. You are not only getting in shape, but you are making the healthy choices of a lifestyle change! This is just one happy circumstance of what adventuring is all about—and you thought this was all about hiking!

Speaking of excuses, the primary excuses are being tired, sore and injured, or, surprise, surprise, all three. Or the coup de grâce of all exercise intentions: "I just don't have the time." What better justification for not getting to the gym or going for a jog (note cynicism here)? Avoiding or working around an injury is a real preoccupation for the older enthusiast of life. Just don't let it get in your way. Rarely will you miss a trip to the gym if you are resolute. In fact, even if you are banged up and on crutches or have an arm in a cast, you can still go to the gym to sit in the sauna or steam room just to keep alive the habit of going to the gym. Rest is also good, but not long-term rest. Therefore, categories of exercise are alternated to allow for recuperation. Soon you will be strong enough and smart enough to avoid injuries and—voilà—you are on the way to being trail ready, or ready for anything. And by the way, your mood should improve, too. You will probably start sleeping and thinking better as well, but that is a theme for another book.

This is not fooling around, either; you need to work up to that hour of honest exercise Monday through Friday. Putzing in the yard or house or walking the dog or hitting a good stride at the mall or, heaven forbid, calling the plays Monday nights does not count. It is cruel advice that someone from the medical community may state that walking a few times a week is enough. I'm here to tell you, and by observing my boomer cohort, once it (fitness) is gone, it is pretty much gone. Then it is all over as life becomes a continuous doctor's visit. Much of this healthy lifestyle "game" is mental.

Exercise Tips from Olympians

The book *Body for Life,* by Bill Phillips, is as good an exercise plan as any. Any plan will do if you stick with it. This is a point of departure to get you exercising, and just as important, to get you investigating what is right for you. *Body for Life* is good mainly because the author took tips from Olympic training, which stressed low weight, high repetition to build muscle and especially tone up while minimizing the chances of injury. I recommend you have the same criteria when you build your knowledge base and select your exercise regimen. What matters is that you settle on a program with the intent that it will be a lifelong pursuit. I found that joining one of the gym chains works for me. That way, I can avail myself of a place to work out no matter where I may be and what workout I may need for the day, whether it is to spin, swim, take a yoga class or two, do CrossFit, or pump some iron. Joining a cycling club is another idea for staying in shape. There are countless biking clubs and offerings from bike shops for all levels of cyclists. I expect most readers will begin with a Google search.

We are spoiled by the internet, but it is smart to build a ready library of exercise and nutrition books. It aids the learning process, which should be augmented by internet searching. There is something right about taking notes, underlining and writing in the margins of the physical page to cement the learning and have it there when it is needed for review.

As with most of the printed word on physical fitness these days, *Body for Life* also hawks a line of pills, potions and supplements, but move past that. The worth of the read is in the very sensible description on *how* to work out. It should be worthwhile, as it has been working for professional athletes and Olympians for years. The Russians "discovered" the very simple methods and advice. Surprise, surprise, it is not about how much weight you lift or how many repetitions you do. It's about how you *warm to the exercise, build to the right amount of weight* and then *push the muscle group to natural fatigue*, at which point it grows stronger. It's all about high reps, low weights and timed sets. Use this method for the various exercise targets you have, whether the goal is flexibility, core, endurance, strength, toning or—best yet—all these goals.

As I discussed earlier, your weekly exercise regimen should vary your exercises, not just to prevent boredom, but to eliminate injuries and achieve better conditioning. The body and mind crave variety.

> **❝ Surprise, surprise, it is not about how much weight you lift or how many repetitions you do. It's about how you *warm to the exercise, build to the right amount of weight* and then *push the muscle group to natural fatigue*, at which point it grows stronger. ❞**

Exercise Intelligently

Get used to working on flexibility by stretching before *and* after every workout. There is a difference: A stretch *before* the workout is for warming up and is not too strenuous. *After* the workout is when you work on flexibility and sink into a stretch facilitated by warm muscles and tendons. Just remember the warm-up needs to be relatively easy, starting with swiveling the head, going through each body section to the feet, and ending with hurdler's stretches for the legs. Do the same to cool down; you will notice more flexibility with warm muscles post-workout.

So many injuries happen with the pre-workout stretch on cold, old muscles and especially tendons. Remember it is normal and natural to lose muscle mass at an accelerating rate as we age. The older body needs time to recover from the rigors of exercise, which is accomplished by varying what you do.

Rather than fight the changes of growing older, honor them. Growing old gracefully is a privilege denied to so many.

What Is a Boomer to Do?

Let's go back to the priorities of physical exercise for the older person: core, which helps with flexibility and balance; aerobic; and anaerobic routines, in that order of importance. Focus on these goals is most important as these capabilities will begin to diminish, some say even in our early 30s. If you focus on the signs of aging—forgetfulness, less strength, less agility, less endurance and diminishing balance—you will be managing them well. Furthermore, while we are talking physical fitness, we are a synergy of body, mind and spirit. Work on one, and the others benefit in a continuous and very happy virtuous cycle.

- *Flexibility and balance*: The best way to gain flexibility and more is by practicing yoga. Yoga builds strength and maintains flexibility and balance. There is a reason it has been around for thousands of years. There is a meditative component to it, but mostly it is about stretching, muscle and endurance building, and training to keep your balance. Also, there is a social aspect, as most yoga these days is done in a class and no one wears orange robes. Try to practice yoga at least twice per week. Yoga can be done as a single workout or after a spin class or resistance workout as a good way to stretch constricted or overused muscles. Yoga is great, as it works on the total body, including digestion, relaxation, sleeping and mental stability, to mention a few of the benefits.

When looking for a yoga class, make sure the instructor understands the older yogi. Younger instructors tend to do extreme poses, which only get older students in trouble, and worse yet, discouraged. Even though every yoga instructor will direct you to "do your own workout," the tendency is to follow the instructor. So, look for an older yoga instructor who gets the needs of the older student and tailors the workout to them. The better instructors will warm the class up gradually, circulate throughout to correct positions, and not do too much or too advanced poses that simply showcase a young, flexible body.

If you do decide to do yoga, give it a good go. Commit to at least six months of a weekly session. It will take time to learn the poses, teach the body new tricks and build the habit of going. You may find, as I have, that you will look forward to class.

- *Core*: A core routine is a series of various crunches, planks, leg lifts and poses with no more than a 5- or 10-pound weight, usually none. A strong core is a bit magical on the effect it can have. If you are human, at some point in your life you will experience back pain, whether it is a short-term pulled muscle, a pinched nerve or something chronic. A strong core prevents these conditions, and it reduces the recovery time. My personal story is that I was diagnosed with age-appropriate lower back pain due to arthritis. Naturally, pills were recommended. I have an aversion to pills, so I asked for a pause in the treatment and started yoga. That was years ago, and the constant nagging in the lower right part of my back is all but gone—all due to yoga. Now, be sensible. Many of us who exercise regularly tend to overdo it or go for a dramatic quick fix. There's no need to go crazy and try an extreme yoga pose; that is a hernia waiting to happen, and it is just *not* necessary. You can find many more suitable and appropriate core-strengthening routines with a simple internet search. And if you're taking a group exercise class such as a spin class, a good instructor can lead a 15- to 20-minute core routine at the end, when you are warmed up. Again, it is much better to do it in a group, as there is "peer pressure" to do a disciplined routine for long enough to get the core, aerobic or anaerobic benefit. This is about age-appropriate conditioning and overall health. Over time, you may even discover the remnants of a six-pack.

- *Aerobic exercise*: Aerobic exercise is good for building your endurance for those long hikes. Steer away from the high-impact exercise you may have done when younger and stick with low-impact alternatives, like swimming, spinning on a stationary bike, as previously mentioned, or gently jogging on a cushioned treadmill. In fact, do all three. Remember, variety is the spice of life, essential to physical conditioning, and keeps your muscles from getting used to any one exercise. Swimming, for example, is all about technique and worth the effort to develop it. A good goal is to work up to a mile—yes, a mile. One of the biggest benefits to swimming is rhythmic, deep, sustained breathing, which we wouldn't do otherwise. It is especially beneficial as our bronchi become less and less elastic with age.

  If you opt to try spinning, look for an instructor who combines a variety of routines matched to the music, which is vital, as the first goal of a beneficial spin is to stay on the beat. The beat determines the intensity of and rest between routines. Hopefully, your instructor will finish with a HIIT (high intensity interval training) routine and cool-down stretch.

  On the treadmill, there is also a proper way to reduce the stress on the joints. Do what is called the "triathlon shuffle." Imagine your feet skimming the surface as you gaze at a single point ahead to keep the body from bouncing up and down, which minimizes the pounding on the joints. Again, do things to make this lifestyle change rewarding. Make note of improvements in general well-being, performance and capability. You may even find yourself taking the stairs two at a time!

- *Anaerobic exercise*: These exercises include resistance and strength training, and it is one of the areas we tend to do incorrectly, so the following section will address the way to do resistance training, respecting the realities of a "seasoned" body.

Doing Resistance Exercises Sensibly

Lifting weights can be seriously dull, tough work, but it is a highly recommended part of conditioning, even if you are not going on an outdoor experience. And lifting weights is only one way to do resistance conditioning: Yoga, core and cross-training offer similar results. Get over the drudgery of this type of training, because done properly it interjects variety and works. I have found that the investment in coaching from a qualified strength and conditioning physiologist (with master's-level education and experience) is worth the expense. You will learn routines and the correct way to pump iron. I was quite surprised and a little amazed that an old-fashioned dead lift is quite technical and nearly a ballet when done right. Why do traditional "weightlifting"? When done right, lifting free weights, bench presses, front and back squats, and deadlifts, for example, involve the whole body, especially the core. And they add the spice of variety to the drudgery of routine exercising.

It is worth reviewing the proven method of lifting weights here. Simply alternate upper body, aerobics and lower-body routines several days per week. Then throw in a little sport or outdoor activity where sweat is required. This is also motivation to eliminate the morning maple twist doughnut because, over time, your body will crave more nutritious and less sweet and salty food to fuel up before and after a workout. You don't want to undo a superior workout, do you?

Always start with a whole-body warm-up that starts from your head and moves throughout the body to your toes. Let's say it's a day you choose to focus on your upper body. You start with chest exercises on a bench press. There should be no more than 30 seconds between sets and no more than a minute between different exercises. This helps the muscles approach fatigue where they will grow in strength. Doing "pyramids," where the weight increases and reps decrease, helps the muscles warm up to slightly more weight. Warming up and gradually moving to more weight is the way to avoid injury. Also, don't be afraid to stop altogether if pain, especially a piercing one indicating a pinched nerve, happens. Move to another muscle group. The phrase "no pain, no gain" is ridiculous, really.

Your first set should be 12 repetitions at a weight that is very comfortable. What happens with this set is that your muscles are told it is time to work, causing blood, and especially electro-chemicals, to increase its flow. This is the beginning of getting age-appropriately "pumped." In the second set, you add slightly more weight and do fewer reps—10, to be exact. The third set is another increment of weight and only eight reps. At this point, it should start being difficult. The fourth set increases the weight and should be reasonably difficult to get in the requisite six reps. For the fifth set, the weight is reduced to facilitate 12 reps. By then, the muscle group should feel fatigued and at a level of real exertion. Rest between sets can be timed with a stopwatch on a lanyard around your neck. But you are not done yet. Change to a different exercise completely, say open chest flies, and put on enough reasonable weight to push the muscle group to exhaustion. Keep rest between reps to 30 seconds and between different exercises to one minute.

Technique is paramount. The object is to only lift the amount of weight that can be done properly, meaning getting a disciplined repetition that exercises the full extension of the muscle group in focus. Pushing a few hundred pounds an inch or two does just about nothing and invites injury.

Make sure you perform a deep, slow, full repetition; down to the count of two, up to the count of one. Inhale on the relaxed part of the repetition and exhale—yes, exhale—on the explosive part of the repetition. When doing a curl, for example, exhale curling up and inhale curling down. In the case of the bench press, breathe in on the way *down* and out on the way *up*. Breathing this way also helps avoid strained muscles, pulled tendons and even hernias.

There are so many neat little tricks on the way to becoming a sensible person. This breathing technique is tough to learn as we, men especially, have been taught to hold our breath and strain the gut when pushing any immovable object. I am constantly and correctly reminded by astute women that men really don't have the corner on brains. No matter who you are, you will probably protest even at the prospect of exercising, let alone learning a whole new way of breathing.[8]

Remember, what was just explained is one take on how to approach exercising. Some routines, CrossFit for example, combine traditional weightlifting and aerobic/anaerobic timed super sets of select exercises of which there seems to be a near infinite selection.

Some of you may read the above and say, "Man, this is not for me, even if I had the time." We remind you again of what Bob Peoples of the Kincora Hostel on the Appalachian Trail observed, "However you get into the outdoors, what matters is you get into the outdoors." Some folks just decide to go for a simple, short hike and do quite well. We are simply suggesting *a* route to fitness, not *the* route for everyone.

Now that we've discussed *how* to exercise, the next progression is to discuss a suggested routine. So, get a good pair of shoes, some cool workout pants and a great wicking T-shirt, and hit the gym with me.

A Week of Exercise: An Example

As we stated earlier, you should alternate your exercises every six weeks to keep your muscles "shocked" into performing. Research shows that muscles get accustomed to similar exercises and plateau in performance and growth after about six weeks of doing the same thing. Some physiologists change a CrossFit routine every time! You must change the types of exercises performed for better results. But this works out well, since doing this helps us get past the boredom that sets in when we do the same thing for too long. It's almost like the body is telling us how to get in shape. I find doing this in a likeminded group provides the motivation to get to the class in the first

---

[8] Get into deep breathing. A good yoga instructor will give you tips on breathing. Do the same breath, no matter the exercise: in through the nose, out through the mouth—slowly, rhythmically, and deeply. It is essential to good oxygen transfer and to keep the bronchi as flexible and efficient as possible, for as long as possible. This is one of the reasons why swimming is such a good life-long exercise; it forces deep breathing.

place and the group motivation to work out diligently.

It bears repeating: The best exercise advice for the older fitness hopeful is to stretch during warm-ups and cool-downs. You will be tempted to skip stretching to save time or because it's boring. But if you don't warm up and cool down properly, you will struggle with or be completely defeated by pulls, strains and damage to the body. And the benefit is not just during exercising; flexible muscles and connective tissue are less likely to suffer from the odd twists and turns of getting through the entire day. I'll bet many readers have horror stories of a back going out while brushing their teeth! If you do not do a few minutes of warm-up and a good five minutes of stretching after a sweat-inducing workout to cool down and keep the body pliable, you are cheating yourself. Keeping the warm-up in mind, what follows is an outline of a weekly full-body regimen:

- **Monday:** *Upper body*: Exercise your chest, shoulders, back, triceps and biceps. Or try a CrossFit class.
- **Tuesday:** *Aerobics*: Use the stair machine for 30 minutes, for example, or take a spin class. A swim is also a good thing.
- **Wednesday:** *Lower body*: Exercise your quads, hamstrings, calves and abdominals.
- **Thursday:** *Aerobics*: Switch it up with 20 minutes on a rowing machine today (20 minutes is the minimum aerobic workout), and combine this with a yoga class.
- **Friday:** *Upper body*: Repeat the Monday routine or do another CrossFit routine. When you get better at exercising, you can vary the routine, even weekly. Notice we have given the upper body four days of ample rest before we exercised this muscle group again.
- **Saturday:** *Aerobics*: How about road biking with the local cycling group or club? Hitting the road with a group is the safest way to do outdoors biking. Make sure you join a "no drop" group so you won't be left behind the pros.
- **Sunday:** *Rest*: Why not rest with your favorite outdoor activity? I personally like a little skeet shooting; it is essentially a very mindful sport.

You may want to add swimming, biking and treadmill jogging to punctuate or augment a variation of the above routine. These three sports comprise a triathlon, which boomers can also do, using much shorter distances as in a triathlon sprint, which is six laps in a pool, a 12-mile bike ride and a 5K jog (just over 3 miles), all on mild terrain, flat and around town. When training for the sprint, add in a yoga session or two, and it will be a welcome break between or in conjunction with your weekday routine. Believe it or not, maintaining a weekly workout will quickly become a regular part of the day if you give it a good go. It's a great motivator to continue regular exercise just to finish one of these sprints, especially if you're over 60. You may find, as I did, that you can finish in the top five in your category of "seasoned" contestants, as there were only six men in the over-60 category. My goal is to periodically do a sprint to celebrate a milestone, such as a reunion or turning 70, until I finish first, simply by outlasting the competition.

Be realistic with your expectations. Don't expect to look like you are ready for a magazine cover. Change is subtle, but change you will (again, sayeth Yoda). Contrary to the outlandish results ("in just 12 weeks") promised in many diet commercials, expect to work at the above schedule for six months. Even then you may not notice much, but someday someone will comment that you look "different, better." Imagine it, and it will happen. Besides, who was the wacko who came up with this "no pain, no gain" nonsense anyway? Pain is pain, and the *end* of gain. No poorer advice was ever given, especially for the older student of a more physically fit lifestyle. Nor is exercise done in a vacuum. It is done while minding lifestyle suggestions that reduce your chronological age, living conservatively with moderation in most things, and, of course, following a sensible diet that includes the occasional slice of pizza and beer, but only after you have made reasonable progress. Sanity is a big part of fitness.

Dealing With Setbacks

It is inevitable that you will have at least sore muscles. But don't let that be an excuse to stop exercising. They will mend shortly, and you can learn to work sensibly around the recovering affliction. If you pull a calf muscle, you can still work upper body and do abdominals. Walk on the treadmill if running exacerbates a pulled hamstring. Don't work the offended muscle group, but move to the sister groups, or in more severe instances, move to the other half of the body.

> **"**There was never a pulled or strained muscle that caused abandonment of a sensible diet and conservative lifestyle habits.**"**

Or simply move in a nonoffending way or in a different direction until the injury heals. Most times, a little exercise is exactly what a sore muscle, sprain or strain needs (if you are unsure about being active with an injury, consult your medical professional; most times you are your own best physician). You can always do something to keep the heart pumping and moving in a generally healthy direction. Also, remember, there was never a pulled or strained muscle that caused abandonment of a sensible diet and conservative lifestyle habits.

There is no secret exercise, machine, diet or formula that is ultimately the way to get in shape. What matters is the individual determination to put together a comprehensive plan and stick to it until it becomes part of you. It's about controlling calories going *in* with a sensible diet and calories going *out* with regular exercise.

Let me mention another reason for all this very tough work and discipline for what may seem so little reward. If we boomers can expect to routinely live into our 90s, how much better it will be to be a vigorous 95 with the trilogy of body, mind and spirit still age-appropriately capable. Remember, you are not working out just to benefit your 50s or 60s; you are also working out to prepare for your vigorous 80s and 90s.

We have talked enough about exercise and diet. You have an idea of what, when and how to do it. It is time to take some action.

> **"**Remember, you are not working out just to benefit your 50s or 60s; you are also working out to prepare for your vigorous 80s and 90s.**"**

Milestones for the Run-Up to the Hike

You should anticipate preparing for your hike for about a year if you are starting out near zero in getting the trilogy together. Let's face it, it has taken you decades to form-fit your La-Z-Boy, and there is a reason they call it a La-Z-Boy (my police friends call it a magic chair because it comes equipped with a beer or two and the remote). It would be unfair to suggest this can be done with an Insanity or CrossFit workout DVD and a mango smoothie every now and again. Start with this plan as a point of departure and elaborate as fits your needs, situation and personality. But let me repeat the cautionary theme: You will plateau, be distracted or just plain discouraged. Fight through it. Share your experiences with like-minded people. Gather strength from knowing what you will be able to do with this newfound health and well-being. Know it is worth the struggle. What follows is the next step in your odyssey, which is to combine body, mind and spirit with getting ready to go on an experience.

One Year Out: Put the Whole-Person Plan in Place

- *Diet*: Tackle this in increments. That is, choose a plan and make it work for a reasonable number of weeks. Take a sanity breather for a day or two when you eat your favorite foods in moderation and return to the plan until you reach a reasonable weight and level of conditioning. Again, remember it is not weight that matters as much as (diet) lifestyle. Try to eat what grows in the earth, not what walks on it. That means shopping around the edges of the grocery store.
- *Lifestyle*: Develop habits for sensible living that help reduce your real age. If you are over 50, get an annual physical. Try to get at least seven hours of good sleep every night. Drive in the slow lane, which is also a metaphor for living. Now is *not* the time to get a Harley. Having one reduces your real age dramatically because they have an inordinate tendency to kill and maim. However, this *is* the time to get a decent road bike and ride regularly with a group.
- *Exercise*: Have a rigorous routine in place. Again, the goal is

honest sweat at least five or six days per week. Refer to the suggested weekly exercise schedule.
- *Goals*: Set short-term goals for diet and exercise, and monitor your progress.
- *Technical competence*: Begin researching your hike. You may want to buy a small library of the best books (naturally, start with *The Honest Backpacker*) and get an appropriate periodical about the kind of hiking you anticipate. Are you a weekender, or are you seeking a distance-wilderness experience? How about checking a local outdoor purveyor like REI or the local college for classes on hiking, trekking or backpacking? Start a three-ring binder to organize all the articles and other information you find so it's in one handy, easy-to-locate place. The first entry should be the hiking prep checklist. And for those who are tech-savvy, journal and collect information electronically. Heaven forbid one has the talent to do so with publishing software. Keeping an electronic "binder" also makes changes, additions and deletions easy.

Six Months Out: Throw in a Little Prep for Actual Hiking
- *Hiking*: Do some day hiking, even if it is in the local park or nature trail.
- *Gear*: Start lists of required and nice-to-have gear. Try some of it out, especially your hiking poles and boots, which must be well broken in before the hike. One with them you must become (Yoda again).
- *Food*: Try a few trail foods when doing the local strolls so you are familiar with what is out there and can prepare a bit for what you will take. Some of the freeze-dried stuff may not agree with you. There is a reason experienced hikers take peanut-butter and marshmallow fluff and bagels or tortilla wraps.

Three Months Out: Transition to Actual Hiking
- *Hiking*: Start regular weekly "hikes" at the local park, on a day hike or on a treadmill with your pack on. Start with an empty pack and graduate to carrying a couple of gallons of water. Rest

assured, hiking with a pack is a different world from what you have been doing. Your center of gravity will be different, and you will find muscles where you never thought you had them.
- *Gear*: You should have all your gear together and be anticipating a dry run overnight, even if it is in the backyard. The tent, for example, will be a bugger to erect the first few times, a chore you do not want to figure out 10 miles into the woods when it may be raining or blowing a gale. Know where you will stow all your stuff in the tent. Practice cooking a meal on the white gas stove. Maybe take a few reads on the compass, which should be used regularly in the woods to orient yourself. Learn how to pack a backpack (see instructions in Chapter 7, "Gear").
- *Food*: You should have a good idea by this stage how you will eat on the trail and how much of it to pack.

Six Weeks Out: Get Trail-Hardened Before You Have To
- *Exercise*: By now, you should be very comfortable with your exercise and diet routines. Your schedule of exercising does not stop; it is augmented with taking trips to the local park for rigorous walks and perhaps day hikes.
- *Hiking*: You should be doing regular pack-on hiking by now. This, too, can be done on a treadmill. Just don't hit the trail with a full pack, even if it is just for the weekend, if you haven't been exercising with it. You will discover new realities with a pack on an hour-long jaunt on the treadmill, even if it is only learning how to adjust it correctly.

Use the above timeline to ease into hiking. Make it your measuring stick. Also, make sure it is flexible because the process will need adjusting as it meets reality.

As mentioned before, trail-hardening *only* happens on the trail. But it can be done in a sensible way, with as much actual hiking and simulated hiking as possible. The very worst thing you can do is assume you can get trail ready on the trail if the trip is for more than a day. You will not make it in one piece. Hiking, especially a distance-wilderness experience, is rigorous, to put it mildly, and more so for the mature hiker.

By now you are coming along nicely with the physical aspect of preparation. It is time to consider the harder work of getting your mind as fit as possible. It is your mind that may be the cruelest enemy of your intentions.

CHAPTER 5
Getting Yourself Ready: Mental Fitness

A person that started in to carry a cat home by the tail was gitting knowledge that was always going to be useful to him.
—Mark Twain

It's hard to get lost on the Appalachian Trail.

This is a voyage of discovery. If you are not having fun, do a reality check, because you should be. When I say fun, I don't mean being giddy all the time. I mean enjoying the huge satisfaction of accepting a challenge and overcoming obstacles. Then there's that thing about being continually awed by nature.

When contemplating an outdoors experience, which is much broader than just going on a hike, you need a general knowledge base and education, plus technical skills. This body of knowledge and competencies will come from books, magazines and the internet, as well as being inquisitive, chatting with folks and trying things out. Try to be purposeful and organized as you accumulate information.

There is a wealth of entertaining and informative books by good writers, which you should read to get different takes on the trail experience. Look for books, like this one, that follow a logical sequence of doing things, stick to facts as much as possible and are practical in application. I personally like books that develop an idea or make a point in an outline form and with bullets. Discard the entertainment/advertising stuff that abounds and zero in on the applicable and informative bits. Goodness knows, don't get your advice from a Saturday morning show on the outdoors, which is mainly an advertisement for a line of clothing or overpriced gear. A good reference book is *The Backpacker's Field Manual*[9] by Rick Curtis. Curtis is succinct, on point and practical, which are virtues in the written word.

After learning the specifics of hiking explained thus far, it's time to soak up some general knowledge and information.

General Knowledge and Education

You will need to build a knowledge base and practical competency about the following areas:
- Equipment and gear
- Staying fed and hydrated on the trail
- The do's and don'ts of camping and traveling in general
- Staying oriented—in other words, not getting lost on the trail
- How to handle possible emergencies and accidents, large and small
- A little first aid

Technical Skills

While you are building a general awareness of hiking, you also need to become technically competent in each of the areas mentioned above, with the specifics dictated by the type of hike you anticipate.

---

[9] *The Backpacker's Field Manual* focuses on wilderness hiking and augments *The Honest Backpacker's* more comprehensive treatment of backpacking, which addresses the more specialized needs of the mature hiker. It is a good backpacking guide—broad in scope while still focused on the essential skills and information that backpackers need to travel safely and comfortably in the wilderness or on a local nature trail.

Simply put, you need to be very comfy with your gear and food (refer to chapters 7 and 8, respectively). For example, it's fine to buy that freeze-dried gourmet food and high-tech backpacking stove at REI, but it's a different thing to be able to fire that puppy up when you can see your breath and the wind is gusting to 20 knots. And it is a far cry from seeing a tent set up on a showroom floor to getting it up and ready for rain and wind on a mountaintop when you are pooped after hiking 12 miles and climbing a few thousand feet of elevation. But don't be discouraged. Routine and experience develop quickly if you are thoughtful and prepared.

- *Equipment*: Refer to Chapter 7, "Gear," for suggestions on equipment categories and choices. Once you have what you need, practice using it until you are good at the function and operation of your equipment as a package. In other words, you should be able to move seamlessly from breaking camp, hiking, making camp, eating and sleeping, and then doing it again in the morning. Ideally, you will have everything you need on your back, because you planned and prepared well. If not, there is the next town to visit. Remember also that the foremost piece of "equipment" is a good hiking buddy.
- *Food*: You need to learn your personal nutrition requirements. Don't go without experimenting and developing the menus most suitable to you before your trip. You must know before you hit the trail which foods will not upset your digestive system, for example.
- *Camping*: Be familiar with leave-no-trace camping in the book (see Appendix 1). It is easy and sensible to do. Begin with good habits so they become routine. The hike is much more satisfying that way.
- *Orienteering*: This means always knowing where you are. Never dismiss the possibility of getting disoriented once you are out of sight of a road or town. The most experienced hikers *always* know where they are and are constantly referring to their maps, properly oriented to the right direction with a compass. I have had the extreme good fortune to experience canoe trips with Burt

Kornegay of Slickrock Expeditions[10]. We would do remote sections of large American rivers like the Rio Grande and the Grand Ronde, where we usually wouldn't see another person for days. Burt, one of the most experienced adventure guides around, kept a waterproof map secured to the gear bags right in front of him for constant reference. He had the whole day of canoeing planned, including stops to eat and rest, sightseeing, and an evening camping spot chosen before we shoved off after breakfast. Thus, you will need to know at least how to read a map with a compass in hand. You can't rely on a GPS because there are situations in which they don't work or you may find the battery has petered out.

A general orientation to the sun is handy, as it usually rises in the east and sets in the west; at night, perhaps know the moon and a constellation or two for navigation. Stay on the designated trail, which, hopefully, is as well-marked as the AT. Just a few skills and common sense make all the difference. Remember you are not developing these skills for when things are going right; you are developing skills and confidence for when things go *wrong*.

- *Emergencies and first aid*: Stuff happens. Hikers get sick and banged up, and shin splints seem to plague the first few days of any hike. Know enough emergency management and first aid to tend to a possible broken bone and the inevitable cuts, scrapes, blisters, sunburn, headaches, insect bites and undiagnosable rashes on your feet. What is most important is to build some sense about how much is enough. Most mishaps won't knock you off the hike, but have brains enough to recognize when a broken bone is not a sprain and get off the trail before you maim yourself. The bone will heal, and you will be back. I hiked with a broken right hand for three days before I had it tended properly. After I fell on it, my able trail mates oooooohed and ahhhhhhed at its swelling and turning black and blue, and then diagnosed it as a sprain and OK for pressing on. Good thing I didn't have a sucking chest wound, which would have no doubt gotten a similar diagnosis.

---

10 Regrettably Burt has retired to work on his many interests, including writing. Happily, he remains a good friend and has given so many people so many life moments, most of all me.

When Enough Is Enough

Finally, know when enough is enough. Most boomers tend to be a little obsessive-compulsive. You can prepare and agonize over every detail and all those "necessary" choices to keep you happily in the process of going hiking but never getting there. There comes a time when you finally need to load up your stuff, strap on your backpack and hit the trail. Nothing will round out your education like a week on the trail, and do try to go for a week if possible. A week is enough time to get into and appreciate a hike. A week provides ample time and certainly a variety of conditions for you to test your physical, mental and emotional preparation. It gives you time to get into a routine of camping, hiking and enjoying splendors galore, whether at your feet or in a valley below. Doing the hike is the ultimate preparation. Set a date and make it happen. As I've said previously, a good rule of thumb is to prepare enough that you are reasonably satisfied with the effort and relatively sure that you will get out and back safely, have fun, and be willing to do it again. And wouldn't it be grand to confidently take a grandchild a few yards into a campsite, not too far from the car, pitch a tent, and cook s'mores on a fire? I personally can hardly wait.

We are progressing resolutely to your goal of getting into nature on a hospitable footing. This section has reviewed trail skills, some of which you are familiar with, and some of which are new, like orienteering. You are becoming well-rounded in your preparations and, I dare say, much more confident in carrying this thing off. The next step is a visit to the doctor if you have not already consulted one early in this process.

A Word About Your Sawbones (Seeing a Doctor, That Is)

Obviously, it is good advice to see a doctor as soon in this preparation process as possible, especially if you have some medical concerns. While this task could have been mentioned earlier, it is discussed here, as seeing a doctor provides mental assurance as much as physical assurance.

As we keep stating, getting ready for an outdoor experience is about gathering information about your whole person—body, mind and spirit. That includes building a long-term relationship with a medical doctor. If you are not seeing one for an annual physical and you are a boomer, start doing so. It's not only a good idea for health, but you need a medical professional who really knows you, mainly for maintenance as you evolve with age, but especially when things go wrong. Think of it as going in for an oil change so your factory mechanic has a chance to monitor that leaky main engine crankshaft seal that is about to go and cause the engine to blow. Besides completing a medical questionnaire for the hike, be prepared to get your money's worth out of the visit by having appropriate questions and a few other things ready (see Appendix 2). Here are some suggestions:

- *Diet*: If you decide to alter your diet or adopt a popular plan to prepare for hiking, jot it down to review with your doctor. If you plan on taking vitamins or supplements, take the packages and bottles with you just to make sure your cocktail won't do more harm than good.
- *Physical fitness*: As with diet, have a training regimen in mind and written down. At least have documented one period of your plans for aerobic, anaerobic, flexibility, core, sports and other activities you anticipate.
- *Health history and medical questionnaire*: Have your doctor prepare a medical questionnaire for you (use the one in Appendix 4). You will want to leave a copy with someone and take one with you, especially if you have a condition that may need attention on the trail.
- *Immunizations*: Are they up to date?
- *Questions and comments*:
    - What is the advisability of you taking [the medicine or pill in question, such as a prescription-strength ibuprofen] on the hike? Get advice on the more powerful medicines you will be taking. Ibuprofen in large doses can kill you by causing bleeding ulcers, so you need to exercise caution. We witnessed this with a young hiker who thought he could control a swollen knee with

800 mg doses of ibuprofen taken twice a day, which didn't help his knee and burned three bleeding ulcers into his stomach. He was 18 hours from death, according to the surgeon who did two procedures on him to stop the bleeding.
- Ask for a refill of any prescriptions; you want an ample supply for your trip.
- Get your doctor's blessing to proceed on your hike.
- If you have any outstanding conditions, ask for a follow-up appointment to monitor progress. At the very least, get on the books for an annual physical. It is a small doable part of lowering your "real age."

While you are considering your medical fitness, make sure you have a health insurance card that is accepted nationally. If your doctor is anything like mine, you will find them most encouraging and helpful. While planning a trip to Belize, my doctor emailed me a profile on indigenous diseases and followed with prescriptions, an injection and advice to be as safe as possible. All this was arranged via the internet because we have a 25-year history; no doctor's visit necessary.

Make sure you keep need-to-know people posted on your progress while preparing for and on the trip. Your doctor may even want a report on how the hike went. One of my doctors expected me to email photos of any fish I might catch.

CHAPTER 6
Getting Yourself Ready: A Fit Spirit

*Experience is the child of thought and
thought is the child of action.*
— Benjamin Disraeli

*An English house on the Coast-to-Coast, probably in the
family for a hundred years or more*

Your first trip is not meant to be some simple rite of passage; it is tough, which makes it worthwhile. If it was easy, anyone could do it. Set small, short-term, realistic, yet challenging goals, and make them happen. Starting with losing a pound or two *is* an accomplishment when that relates to either reducing the weight of your pack or reducing your waistline. Then move to the next pound or two if that is what you want to do. Realize that you don't have the wind you used to as a teenager. Still, be prepared to take credit for and enjoy some vim and vigor returning.

What I mean is that you gather the energy to do something worthy by summoning the collective power of body, mind and spirit, which when combined become the proverbial "greater than the sum." You will know it when it happens: A tough workout becomes a breeze. You reach a weight-loss target. You feel energized when waking in the morning. You look forward to the rigors of the hike or whatever undertaking you are contemplating.

You are becoming a more interesting person!

Spiritually, the zest for life is probably the most important part of the trilogy. We are talking about developing enthusiasm, which engenders discipline and a work ethic to make a hike memorable, or at least an activity you will want to replicate. This inexorably leads to other interests, people and certainly places you may never have considered, even while leafing through the latest *National Geographic*. As the ancients advised, the way to understand life is by understanding yourself. By going through this process, you will learn much about who you are; keep the good and improve the bad. The prospects for self-improvement, adventure and meaningful occupation increase in number and grow organically at nearly a geometric rate—that is, doubling regularly, or so it seems.

Make a plan that moves toward your goal, no matter what it may be, and *stick to it* by any means or trick you can employ. But be realistic. Your goal is to be *fit*, not buff; do the reading and study to be *technically prepared*, not expert in every detail; and dream about possibilities to remain involved and be *excited* about an activity in which it is easy to become enthusiastic. There are so many unpredictable, unexplainable good things and remarkable people that happen on and off the trail that it just must be experienced. Friendships of a lifetime will be formed if only by having similar interests, and certainly by the time you spend a night on the trail with an intrepid buddy.

> **"**Your goal is to be *fit*, not buff; do the reading and study to be *technically prepared*, not expert in every detail; and dream about possibilities to remain involved and be *excited* about an activity in which it is easy to become enthusiastic.**"**

Dream a little with me . . . There is nothing quite as motivating as a dream or two. But make sure you make a few happen. Learn to say *yes* to suggestions from friends and acquaintances, even if it's to skydive or hike to villages around Mount Everest with Sherpas and yaks. Dabble in a bit of the exotic: If you have always wanted to sail a tall ship, for example, this is your chance.

Reward yourself with treats after your preparation for a hike and dreams of more adventures at the end of the hike. If the treat is high in calories, remember to practice moderation. Go to a movie with your favorite companion and share some popcorn to celebrate swimming your first quarter mile. Make that trip to the Spanish Riviera happen. The fact is, once you begin seeing possibilities, one leads endlessly to another and another.

Then there is the option of variety to spice things up. Worlds will open. There are sports, biking, hiking, and canoeing clubs, fishing clubs, kayaking, ecotourism, agri-tourism, equestrian tourism, safaris with white tablecloths, luxury barges down famous rivers, fishing for peacock bass on the Amazon . . .

Pick something physical to do on your day of "rest" or on those days that the exercise routine doesn't happen or an injury keeps you off the treadmill for a few days. (By the way, there is a reason a treadmill is called a treadmill; it is rather monotonous. Make sure to use a music player to liven things up.) There is nothing wrong with picking up the old racquetball racket again. Just make sure you participate and not watch. One never ceases to marvel how many millions of experts there are on football who have never played the game. What could be better than to be vital and vigorous enough to play football when you are north of 60, even if it is flag football in your backyard with several generations of family?

Always contemplate the positive as a defense for when the negative thought or happening creeps into your life or your psyche. Moving resolutely to a state of physical and mental readiness to do something as rigorous as a distance-wilderness hike makes you healthy, well-rounded and more content with your situation in life simply by the pursuit of the goal of taking a hike. You will have fewer and fewer injuries. Colds and upper respiratory problems will lessen or be all but eliminated. You will indeed be rolling your "real" age back to what it can be. Can you roll it back five or six years earlier than your actual age? That is realistic.

And keep your eyes on the hiking prize. You *will* experience life as you never have. You *will* learn more about yourself and others—and mostly good things at that. You *will* become a much more interesting person. You *will* develop other interests and occupations. You *will* open other doors. You *will* resurrect intentions and make them happen. You *will* learn things to pass on to children and grandchildren, whether or not they are yours.

Pause for a moment and write your own paragraph to continue this one. Just how do you imagine your life playing out?

PART III: PACKING ESSENTIALS

Don't tell my wife, but I just now have her convinced that her pack is all volume and not weight.
—Anon

(TRUE QUOTE FROM A MAN HIKING AHEAD OF HIS WIFE, WHO CARRIED A BIGGER PACK THAN HE DID. THEY WERE BOTH SMILING, LUCKILY FOR HIM.)

A view from the trail on the England Coast-to-Coast hike

The Honest Backpacker

It takes a lot to maintain our lives, yet we take it all for granted: the convenience of a roof over our heads that hopefully doesn't leak, transportation at the ready in the garage, food at a nearby grocery store, and an urgent care for every little ache and pain. We are also able to stay dry when it is wet, cool when it is hot and warm when it is cold. And we don't have to hike up and downhill a half mile for a drink of water, which must be purified before quenching a cotton mouth. It is a whole other consideration when your hearth and home is on your back, and a good pair of socks and boots are the only things between you and the next camp.

What follows is more than a list of handy things to pack in a backpack; it streamlines what and how to pack. There are oodles of references that tell you how to do this, but this is a reference from the perspective of mature hikers who were nearly finished with an AT thru hike. Man, they had it down—and they had it good. They cut their combs in half to cut down on weight, yet they had the pleasure of fresh, hot blueberry muffins for dinner on a mountain-top of heart-quickening camaraderie, beauty and serenity. So, let's get packing.

CHAPTER 7
Gear

*Imagination grows by exercise, and contrary to common belief,
is more powerful in the mature than in the young.*
—W. Somerset Maugham

All the gear for a wilderness backpacking experience

If you pack what all the outfitters, "experienced" hikers and books recommend, you will need at least one stout-hearted Nepalese Sherpa and his good-natured yak. Initially, the stuff you will want to pack is dizzying in volume and variety. But what you must have on a summer trip in the lower 48 will round off to about 30 pounds, especially after the first 10-mile day. Just think about the daily activities you will be doing in the wild—mainly eating, drinking (and the result thereof), sleeping and hiking—and then prepare accordingly. If you think you may not use it, you probably won't.

Gear does not include food, though food weight is considered in that target pack weight of 30 pounds. This list is only one take on what is generally packed on a distance-wilderness hike (a trip of more than 50 miles). Just pack a little less food if you plan an overnighter.

This suggested list is for a summer outing. Naturally, tolerance for heat, cold, wet and dry is up to you. This equipment is meant for temperatures above 40 degrees at night. So, pack and conduct business to prevent heat exhaustion during the day and hypothermia at night or when the temperature may drop. Even in the summer you will be wet from sweat, so wind protection is important to ward off the chilling effect of that wind, especially at altitudes where there may be a wind chill factor. Always keep your pack, food, sleeping bag, sleeping clothes and a change of clothes, especially socks, dry.

Be advised, don't go on a trip with new equipment. If anything is even just a little off, like your pack or shoes, it can make the entire trip unpleasant. Even a small ill-adjustment to a hip belt will eat a hole in your hip/leg joint and cause undue torture. I speak from experience on this one. The list on the following pages should only guide your selections. Make your own "to-buy" lists from these suggestions.

Don't forget to shop wisely. We found the big chains were helpful. Make sure you have some study under your belt *before* you visit an outfitter. We realize that many folks go to a good outfitter for their great advice and service and then shop online only to save a few dollars. That is just not kosher! We all need to be frugal and, realistically, your gear will come from multiple sources. But if you get advice and service from an outfitter, do them the courtesy of also purchasing there. We not only got several painstaking fittings from the manager where we purchased our packs, but we also got impeccable service after a shakedown trip where we found out the backpacks were not exactly right. The manager sent the packs back to the manufacturer for some major modifications . . . all at no cost to us.

Don't go cheap; you usually get what you pay for. Don't buy the first thing you see. Get the good, light, durable stuff. And know how each piece of your equipment performs. Do a dry run with everything under actual conditions until you are comfortable with it.

Some things can be purchased at discounters or at a used sports equipment shop. You may even consider renting just to see what all the hubbub is about. Be aware that renting is quite expensive, but then again, a full pack of really neat stuff sitting permanently in the attic is quite pricey too. At the time of this writing, expect to pay just north of a thousand dollars for everything, even for the good stuff, plus incidentals to and from the local trail. But once you are outfitted, backpacking is a convenient and inexpensive getaway or vacation that takes a whole lot less muss and fuss than doing the hotel thing. I say hotel because day hikes from B&B to B&B are fabulous. A hot bath, a good meal and a real bed are quite the reward for a day of hiking. And a day pack is a whole lot lighter than a backpack. At the other extreme, backpacking can be as simple as a Saturday night at the nearby bass lake or trout stream, which can be had for next to nothing once you are up and running.

Essential and Optional Gear

Remember Me and You, the trail names of the AT thru-hikers extraordinaire? They had packing down to a science. The **bolded items** (covered in the sections on pages 92 through 113) indicate the gear that Me and You had in their packs after 1,700 miles, and about 500 to go. Consider a bolded item mandatory or close to it, with everything else optional. I thought the reader would like to learn from other experienced hikers, especially two who successfully completed one of the most demanding hikes in the world. At 1,700 miles, Me and You were still concerned with shedding gear to save weight, having shed all the body weight they physically could. They were doing quite well, with less than 35 pounds in their heaviest pack, including pillows and a journal carried by Me, or was it You? The other pack, which the Mrs. carried, was less than 25 pounds and getting lighter. One more thing: They were both rather slight people but handled these weights quite casually. Now let's see how they easily and efficiently put all their needs on their backs every morning.

The Backpack

Backpack manufacturers seem to be continually improving their products, and for good reason. Next to a knowledgeable hiking buddy, great boots and agile hiking poles, your backpack is the most important piece of equipment, in my estimation. The range of choice is dizzying. There are packs for every size, shape and sex. Take your time. This piece of equipment must be right.

HOW TO PACK A BACKPACK

The illustration below shows the suggested way to pack a backpack:

Horizontally: Distribute weight and bulk equally.

Vertically: Keep the heavy stuff, such as food and water (bladder), on the top, next to the body. Use the outside pockets for frequently used items, especially water, maps, rain gear and a camera.

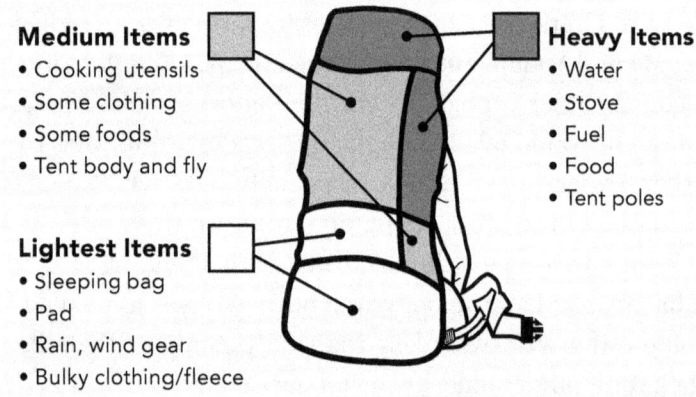

Medium Items
- Cooking utensils
- Some clothing
- Some foods
- Tent body and fly

Heavy Items
- Water
- Stove
- Fuel
- Food
- Tent poles

Lightest Items
- Sleeping bag
- Pad
- Rain, wind gear
- Bulky clothing/fleece

- *Backpack*: A 3,200-cubic-inch (ci) internal frame is ideal for a 50-mile trek, though you may want a bigger pack to be roomy enough for other purposes, rather than getting different packs for different hikes. Winter, for example, requires more stuff.
- *Stuff sacks*: Have a bag each for food and clothing. You may want to color-code them to make it easy to grab the right sack the first time. They only need be as big as necessary for the contents,

which is smaller than you think. Some experienced hikers use plastic grocery bags for food and hang them from the shelter on the pre-existing mouse-proof hangers. Ask the folks on the trail and/or in town if it is necessary to hang a bear bag; mice are usually a much bigger worry, as they are relentless at getting to your food, and they have learned to hang around campsites and shelters.

- ***Pack cover***: This usually can be ordered with the pack; use it. It should be kept in one of the external pouches with your ultralight waterproof windbreaker, ready to cinch over your pack and you when rain suddenly hits. Keep your pack dry! Cover it at night if left outside your tent. Even dew is no good; if your stuff is wet, it will be heavier. Some hikers keep their pack in the tent if clouds are forming. The prevalence of mice will determine much of how you store food and gear for the night. Remember, mice make their living on the trail, and they are smarter, faster, heartier and braver than you are.
- ***Baggies***: One-gallon or two-quart sizes are adequate. These are for keeping individual portions of food dry and contaminant-free, as well as for your first aid kit, hygiene kit, thunder tree kit (toilet paper/handi wipes/antibacterial hand sanitizer), camera, etc. Don't forget the rubber bands, as the zip-locks tend to lose their locking ability, especially after a few uses.

Sleeping: To Tent or Not to Tent?

Your tent, lines, pegs and ground cover go in the stuff sack that comes with the tent. Your sleeping bag has its own stuff sack. Some plastic-bag their tent and then put it in a stuff sack, especially if traveling on or near water is part of the trip. Both of those go in the bottom of your pack. The sleeping pad is strapped on the outside for access during the day. Your optional pillow goes somewhere inside the pack away from the body on an outer surface, preferably directly away from the upper back to keep it away from sweat. Or you can stuff extra clothes in a stuff sack for a pillow. Make sure this makeshift affair goes under the sleeping bag, as a bare stuff sack tends to stick to your face, just for an added challenge to sleeping.

- **Tent**: Your tent should be easy to assemble and disassemble and withstand tons of abuse while keeping wind and rain out. Make sure your tent is sealed with seam sealer at least twice. And make sure you set it up multiple times in the living room, backyard or local park *before* you hit the trail. Set all the lines, including ones for the rain fly, and stakes to ensure they work. Do it as many times as it takes to learn how to do it quickly and with confidence. An experienced rigger never misuses or steps on his lines. Think about it: It is more than a superstition born of sailors who, from brutal experience, knew that every line had to be treated with discipline and respect, lest it fail at a moment of truth. Distance hikers aim for shelters and don't use tents, but you must have your stuff together for this hardy tactic. Some distance hikers use a hammock instead of a tent, but a hammock still requires a fly and perhaps mosquito netting, as well as a couple of trees, and then having to do it all in the wind—so *fageddaboudit*.
- **Plastic moisture barrier**: This is the first thing between the ground and your tent. Don't think you can do without this because your sleeping gear, especially your sleeping blanket, will absorb ground moisture. Put loops of line on each grommeted corner of the moisture barrier to loop over tent poles, which will stretch it flat and keep it under your tent, not bunched between your shoulder blades.
- **Sleeping pad**: Keep your sleeping pad rolled up and lashed externally on your backpack, where it is handy for a noon snooze.
- **Sleeping bag**: Make sure it is weighted for the season. Some summer hikes only require a sleeping bag liner (see the next point). Obviously, the conditions of the hike and time of the year will dictate what you get. Spend some time on getting the right match and a quality bag. This is another area where it doesn't pay to be cheap. There is nothing as miserable as being too cold or too hot when other things are conspiring to keep you from sleeping. And you can't just layer on more clothing if the winds whip up at night—it doesn't work. The sleeping bag must always be kept dry, so pack it in a large garbage or leaf bag before you stuff it in

your pack. Compress it and wrap it with ties for compactness. The mummy style is good, but get the next taller size to yours, as it really is a mummy and fits very snugly. If you get your size, you won't be able to turn and you will be uncomfortable all night. I, for one, prefer to move in my bag.
- *Sleeping bag liner*: This is for longer trips and colder weather. Or it can be used instead of a bag in warm conditions, as mentioned above.
- **Inflatable/collapsible pillow**: There are many, but Therm-a-Rest has served me well. If it is ultralight, a lot of experienced hikers take this luxury. It is one of the few concessions of weight to civilization and humanity, besides coffee, that is forgivable.

Carrying everything for body and soul on one's back and being completely prepared is, at least to me, a great experience and an even greater confidence builder in general. Next, consider eating.

Getting Ready to Eat: Fire, Pot and Spoon

After the first few days or so, when you may not have an appetite, your hunger kicks back in and even the plainest food is most satisfying. Everyone develops their own trail menu, so the only universal wisdom is to keep "fueled." Your body is taking a remarkable pounding, so it's important that you eat regular meals, drink plenty of water and get enough rest. Your body will tell you what it needs if you pay attention.
- *Stove*: We believe a stove is mandatory, as there is something right and soothing about hot food and coffee or chocolate, or both for a mocha. Although some weight freaks go cold to save the weight of cooking paraphernalia, there are many options here. Again, the choice will be dictated by conditions; for example, do you bring a stove when there will be plenty to eat along the chosen path? If you bring one, do you need a windscreen to conserve fuel? Stoves are simple because they need to be. When we stopped at a hostel on one trip, a fellow hiker made an adequate stove out of a Coke can. First, he cut it in half, then he perforated the bottom of the bottom half with his pocketknife. The top of the can then became

the bottom of the stove, which he stuffed with cotton to absorb and meter the fuel for burning. He then turned the former bottom half of the Coke can into the half stuffed with cotton and fuel, and the stove was ready to light, which he did with a flourish and proved its worth by heating some water.

The denatured (see below) alcohol-burning Trangia, one of many good stoves, is so small it seems too cute to be of service, but it blasts morning coffee water or the evening rehydrated teriyaki chicken. Consider purchasing a windshield, even though it is a pain to set up. It conserves fuel and allows extended and concentrated heat for a treat of fresh-baked goods. If you decide to go with cold food, then the stove and all its accoutrements are not needed. However, a hot cup of morning coffee is quite satisfying, as is hot soup after a day of hiking.

- ***Fuel***: Put denatured alcohol in a sports bottle that seals tightly. The metal bottle looks cool but weighs too much. Take just a little more fuel than you think you need. A denatured stove is better for warmer hikes because of its fuel properties. Cold temperatures affect alcohol mainly because it is more difficult to light when cold, as it takes on the ambient air temperature. Still, it is the preferred stove if you need a stove at all, since you will quickly learn how to light it under all conditions. Some campers put the bottle in their sleeping bag at night to have it warm in the morning. Another fact of the trail is that you burn much more fuel on the trail than you might while trying out your newest toy in the comfort of your kitchen, where there is no wind. It is common to use the entire fuel reservoir heating the morning 16-ounce ration of water for a hot beverage and cereal. So, try to shelter your stove from the wind when you can.
- ***Fire***: Get a good brand-name lighter. Cheap ones tend not to light when damp, even from dew. Then have waterproof matches handy. As I said above, cold denatured alcohol is difficult to light. When it is cold, you must put the flame right on the fuel and hold it till it slowly takes. In fact, you must feel where the flame should be, briefly, to determine if the stove is fired up because you can't

readily see the flame. And it may sound obvious, but don't do this in or even near your tent. It is just a matter of time before the stove tips over, and a tent is highly flammable.

- *Cookpot/cup combo*: For space-saving purposes, make sure your lone cookpot (one is plenty) is large enough to hold your stove and lighter. It should be titanium, since it is superlight and most durable. You want to be able to boil 16 ounces of liquid with enough room to stir in a dehydrated dinner. Also, when the stove is finally lit, the flame is nearly invisible, so burns come easy. The handle on even the snazziest cookpot is made to get screaming hot, hot enough for branding, but not cherry red, so it remains very innocent looking—what a clever trick. Be very careful to treat everything you cook with as if it is hot; a burn on the trail is miserable, so use your bandanna for a potholder. You will learn this lesson very quickly.
- *Lexan spoon*: This is all you need (except a small pocketknife). Some campers cut the handle down for storage and weight-reduction purposes. Did I say weight is an obsession? Well, it will be if you spend more than a night or two camping and hike more than 5 or 10 miles with an overweight backpack.
- *Cup*: Splurge on titanium here also. It is nice to drink that mocha while your pre-portioned Cream of Wheat, brown sugar, protein, dried fruit and slivered almonds warm to perfection. Notice that I didn't say granola . . . *bad granola*! Granola may have an adverse effect on the digestive system, and you don't want to be asked to hike last in line.
- *Camp sponge*: Sounds strange, but you need something to clean pots and pans and wipe down the gear before it is packed for each day's hike. Boy Scouts have been known to use a pine cone, but a sponge works a whole lot better. Keep it in the pot with the stove and the lighter.
- *Fry pan*: This is optional, depending on whether you want to do some baking. This also means you will need cooking oil, which adds more weight, implies you will be cooking more often, and means more food stuffs need to be hauled—now you are talking

a whole different kind of camping. That's not necessarily a bad thing. Even a French coffee press has its place on the trail, but now we are talking about a different kind of hiker, too, one who likes their creature comforts. I have a friend who hauled a small picnic table to a remote trout stream so he could serve a checkered tablecloth dinner of fresh trout in the middle of the flowing water to his daughter. Now, there's a guy who knows how to do camping; she never forgot that trip—and neither did he.

- *Cooking utensils*: Take a plastic spatula or spoon only if you plan on doing a little frying or baking. Naturally, cut the handles down to fit in the fry pan and, you guessed it, to save weight.

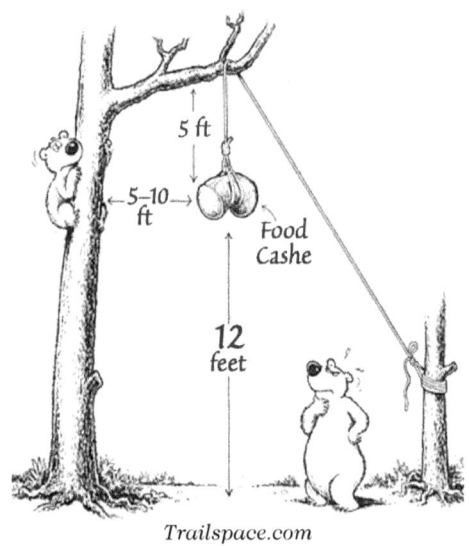

Trailspace.com

- ***Bear bag***: You may need to hang your food where the critters can't get to it. The bear bag can also be your food bag. Again, check local conditions. Bears may not be a concern. A bigger concern is the mighty mouse—if you see even one, that means the entire delegation is right behind. Back to the bears: A bear bag should be hung between two trees, with one rope over one limb and another over a second tree limb to pull it to the side and thus suspend it a good 12 or so feet off the ground. Can you imagine the bear that can reach a Butterfinger more than three yards in the air?

- ***Carabiner***: This is to sling the bear rope over a limb. You may want to just rely on a local rock or stick tied to the end of the rope. We've also seen hikers put stones in a small cloth bag that previously held a pair of sunglasses, and use that for slinging the line. That's taking saving weight to the Nth degree.
- ***Rope***: It is handy to have a frugal length of lightweight cord, especially if a bear bag will be hung. One 30-foot length of 550 parachute riser cord (no smaller than a quarter-inch thick) is great, or perhaps two lengths, depending on how you will hang your bear bag.

With eating, must come drinking, which one must do frequently and safely, free from contaminants. So, water, our next concern, must be ample, readily available for a swig while in motion, and quite pure.

Hydration

Mark Twain's wisdom seems never out of place. While he was probably alluding to drinking something other than water, let's assume he is observing that when hiking you must hydrate frequently and with purified water. Again, I digress; let's continue the book.

> *Water, taken in moderation, cannot hurt anybody.*
> —Mark Twain

Hiking is a series of essentials—eating, drinking, sleeping, sanitation—that are accommodated by routine and good habits. Just as establishing a regular process for making and breaking a leave-no-trace camp, purifying water and ample hydration need to be equally routine. All it takes is one time for you to not purify that crystal-clear, cool mountain water when microbes are present, and—bam!—you're talking amoebic dysentery or giardia. Not pleasant.

- ***Bottles (two each)***: A word to the wise: Use Nalgene bottles only for a short hike. They're sturdy and just about indestructible, but sports drink bottles work just as well—and you save an eye-popping 10 ounces. Just remember to keep those sports bottles in the pack's external pouches in case one is damaged; you don't want

wet gear. Also, they need to be handy for a swig on the go.
- ***Platypus***: The platypus is a bit of a universal term for a low-profile hydration system made to fit in a panel in a backpack. Its main feature is a tube that is fastened to a front shoulder strap for immediate, convenient access so it is easy to keep hydrated. This is an alternative to the "hog-snout" bladder (see below). It's your choice, but you need one or the other. The hog-snout is more versatile, and it can be suspended from a tree trunk to make it a sort-of shower.
- *Water bag ("hog snout")*: The hog snout is a nickname for a water bag with a valve that is reminiscent of a pig's nose. The MSR 4-liter bag is respectable. One fill in the evening can be used for supper, a "shower," breakfast and the morning's hiking water till noon. Plan to stop to refill your water containers so you don't have to carry the full bladder. Always remember to purify the moment a container is filled.
- ***Purification***: Tincture of iodine works in a pinch, but with a bit of a medicine taste, which is not too bad if you're thirsty. SweetWater-brand purifier did well for us. Two drops of bleach per liter also does the trick; keep it in an old eye-drops bottle. It will be enough to last the longest of hikes. Whatever you do, be sure to use purification, no matter how clear and cool the water seems, and even if it is "only just a small taste."

Clothing: Lightweight and Just Enough

While the list of clothing that follows seems lengthy, it tucks neatly in your pack, and you will be warm enough when it is cold, cool enough when it is hot and dry enough when it is wet.

We are considering a summer hike on the AT where the days are hot and the nights are warm, so the clothing recommendations reflect that. Outdoor clothing has come a long way since ol' Levi put his canvas tents to better use. Ripstop pants are quite tough, those wicking T-shirts really work, and the right boots are a marvel of fit and function. While laboring up a few thousand feet of altitude, I noticed what appeared to be frost as I looked down the front of my pricey Capilene T-shirt. It was sweat being "pulled" from my body to evaporate and cool me just as advertised. It is neat when a product performs the way they say it should.

- **Shoes, plus inserts**: Break in the shoes very well. Wear them for several weeks or until the fit is perfect; that means no hot spots after rigorous hoofing. Inserts are for better instep support (I use Superfeet), but you can forget them unless your trial runs tell you they are needed. If your boots are advertised as being waterproof, then test that theory. But even if they are, you should waterproof them anyway to make sure they keep water out, as wet feet are uncomfortable and prone to diseases like jungle rot. A few coats should do the job. Gore-Tex-lined boots are great, but they take quite a while to dry out the sweat at night—hence the need to do a waterproofing treatment on your own. Shoes are another area you do not want to skimp on. That's why they are listed in the number-one spot. They are all that's between you and the trail. Make sure the laces are kept in good shape, but your bear-bag parachute cord makes a good lace in a pinch. Long-distance hikers break in two pairs of trail boots, one for reprovisioning along the way in the event the first pair wears out, like they will while doing the AT, for example.
- **Socks**: Take two pairs of the wicking style. Keep them both as dry as possible. Some folks tie yesterday's pair to the outside of the pack after washing to gather a little sun. Turning them inside out also works in a pinch.
- *Sock liners*: Again, get the wicking ones; this is optional depending on your trial run.
- **Shirt, long-sleeve**: Make sure it is wicking material again. A Simms SolarFlex[11] long-sleeve pullover shirt isn't cheap, but get one anyway. They are like a second skin in comfort, they have super sunblock capabilities, and they are wicking. Worth the price. You may want a light color so you can identify ticks quickly. Consider a sun-repellent, long-sleeve shirt, as even the deep woods have bald areas where the sun is intense. On the hike across England, we were in a whiteout near Hadrian's wall, and our hands got quite sunburned as

---

11 https://www.simmsfishing.com/

we trekked across the fabulously purple-heathered moors.
- **Shirt, long-sleeve buttoned**: Think about a Simms Guide shirt or two. You will love your Simms shirts, which are stylish, tough, and above all, functional.
- **T-shirt**: Wicking, of course. The new-generation fabrics, like Capilene, are a little expensive but worth it because they work as advertised by wicking away sweat, which acts as a coolant, and some have UV protection. The Patagonia silk-grade Capilene, for example, looks so good it can be worn to church after the hike. Depending on the weather, you'll want three of these puppies, with one reserved for sleeping; you just don't want to sleep in your hiking tee.
- **Sweater**: Another layer of warmth is smart, and a lightweight fleece will do it. Naturally, it is weather-dependent. If you are gaining any altitude, factor in that mornings may be a little colder.
- **Jacket**: Get something light, windproof and waterproof. This type of jacket will not be cheap, but bite the bullet. REI has good-quality gear, and they stand by it. I took back a windbreaker after some use because I ripped the sleeve. REI replaced it on the spot, and only subtracted a little discount for use up to the time of the damage. You need wind protection more than you need rain protection while on the trail because you will already be wet from exuding those noxious bodily residues; a good windbreaker will keep you warm. Plus, you can get hypothermia at altitude, even on a warm day, so remember to layer, which you may have to do even in August when you are at 6,000 feet.
- **Underwear**: Take two or three pairs of whatever you're comfy in. Some outfitters will recommend synthetic ones. You be the judge. If you have been wearing cotton Jockeys all your life, they're fine for the trail as well. Those with larger thighs have learned to use a Slick Stick or Vaseline to avoid chafing.
- **Sleepwear**: Consider silk-weight, very light long johns for sleeping. Your very worn-in PJ bottoms and a T-shirt work as well. It is a choice between the added weight and comfort. I like nightwear, as I don't like the feel of a sleeping bag. Also, with PJs you can sleep

on top of the sleeping bag quite comfortably. Professional guides and military survivalists suggest going naked, as sleeping bags are designed to use your body heat, which can't be done as well when you are dressed. If you choose to do this, check for ticks before you zip up. Burt Kornegay, our wilderness guide extraordinaire, simply stretched out in his sleeping bag liner in the bottom of his canoe most nights and slept like a baby. As part of your preparation, you will check the weather, which will make the decision for you about what to sleep in. Temps in the 40s seem to mandate warmer sleeping gear. Again, avoid cotton garments in favor of the ultralight wicking materials.

- *Pants*: Get the *ripstop* kind that convert to shorts, even though you will most likely keep the lower legs on, as they take the place of gaiters. Still, some folks prefer shorts. If so, you will need some sort of gaiter for protection from supernaturally mean trailside foliage and jumping, pointy, possessed rocks that defy gravity to get into your boots.
- *Pants, second pair*: Take a second pair of *ripstop* convertible pants/shorts, which have many occasional uses, if only to go to town or have something to wear while the first pair is being washed.
- *Hat*: This is a personal choice. But once you try a Tilley, an expensive hat recommended by dermatologists, you will not go back.[12] It is broad-brimmed, keeps the sun off, floats, is indestructible, and looks cool with your clip-on sunglasses riding jauntily on the side. Most folks take their favorite ball cap, but we just don't need that much sun. Oil of Olay can only do so much after the big "5-0."
- *Sunglasses*: These are a must-have for this author, made mandatory by years in the sun on the farm and elsewhere. The eyes tell you when you've had enough glare and UV light, because, at least with me, my eyes have a sand-in-the-eye feel and begin to water the minute the sun rises and I am heading into it.

---

12 A note from Crackerjack: Tilley rhymes with silly, which is defined in his book as a cheap hat with a broad brim that can be found at any store. It protects well but looks silly in photographs. A Tilley is not cheap, but it's another item worth the cost. My Tilley goes on every hike. Plus, there is a no-fault policy: If you lose it or it's destroyed somehow, proof of purchase will get you 50 percent off the new one. No hassle. They are legendary in their durability. A zookeeper had one pass through an elephant several times, and it was good as new after a quick run through the washing machine. There's even a cool pouch in the liner for an ID card and a $20 bill for emergencies.

- **Camp shoes**: Get Waldies camp shoes or Crocs with a heel strap. They are light, indestructible and a relief at the end of the day when the boots just must come off. You need the strap to keep them from floating off your feet when you take a dip in a river. Whatever you do, don't take shower flip-flops. Believe it or not, they are heavy, and what's more, they just don't work; they float away when "dancing with trout."
- **Gaiters**: These are optional. Better to take convertible long-legged pants and just not remove the legs. There is just too much stuff that jumps into your boots or filets the bare leg. However, on established trails, such as the AT, you are not bushwhacking. The AT is hindrance-free almost all the time, and so was the C2C.
- **Hankies**: I'm not talking about a bandanna. This is a hankie, like your dad used to keep in his breast pocket. Keep your hankie as clean as possible for cleaning glasses and the like. A bandanna is used for the rough stuff, like as a potholder. Go ahead and soil your bandannas, no problem; you can give them a quick swoosh and a rinse in any creek to keep them clean enough.
- **Bandannas**: Take two. One needs to hang from your pack, ready to mop your brow dozens of times a day. Use them for potholders, water filters, bandages and a thousand other things. We recommend you use one for a potholder on the first day and burn a nice big hole in it, just to get it over with.
- **Swim trunks**: These are optional depending on the modesty of the hikers in question. Some hikes afford the luxurious dip in a hot spring. Then there's always the need for a bath of opportunity along the way in that babbling brook. It's icy cold but such a pleasure when under a canopy of hardwoods and surrounded by nothing but the best of nature.

Barring the most unfortunate circumstance where you become violently sick or injured, you won't need much by way of attending to minor maladies. You will be most pleasantly surprised that all your first aid needs fit in a quart-size plastic baggie.

First Aid: All That Will Fit in a Plastic Baggie

Your first aid kit is a personal thing. But there are a few essentials to keep in mind. More than what's listed, give or take an item or two, what you take is a matter of choice between real need, convenience, overkill and weight. You could share an item, for example; why should two people need more than one pair of scissors? A good sharp knife is usually all you need for cutting and trimming. It bears repeating that what you take can be worked out during your training and preparation period. Everyone tries to anticipate every malady, all mayhem and mishaps galore. The health-supplies manufacturers are all too happy to oblige this apprehension with all sorts of first aid kits, some of which take a bit of medical training to use. Again, be prepared, but there is no need to go overboard. A quick Google search will get you plenty of advice on how to pack one or get one prepackaged. We found it better to pack our own, as everyone has preferences for first-line medical treatment.

- *Neosporin*: The first aid kit in a tube. Don't leave home without it. We put this first, as it has so many applications that it approaches magic. I wonder what they put in it, like the main ingredient in WD-40 is fish oil . . . but I digress.
- *Band-Aids*: Take an assortment; leave the can or box behind. They now have liquid Band-Aids to paint over a cut, which is quite nice; will wonders never cease?
- *Ibuprofen*: Try to get prescription-strength 500 mg pills or better, then put a nice handful in a small pill bottle. Be aware of the side effects of ibuprofen and medicate responsibly. Think about that morning and evening preventive maintenance pill for the first week as a simple relief for sore muscles. Don't stay on it too long; it can irritate the stomach.
- *Tylenol*: This is for headaches, just like the advertisement says, but if you prefer, ibuprofen may be all you need for headaches, too.
- *Imodium A-D*: Bring some along just in case your stomach acts up. Note: Don't let folks share your edibles with their bare hands. Always share by pouring stuff in their mitts or using *your* hands; hey, what are friends for?

- ***Antibiotics***: When you get your medical checkup, ask about getting some. Again, understand appropriate dosages and when it should be used.
- ***Moleskin, Compeed or blister packs***: When you develop a hot spot, usually on your feet, it must be attended to right away! A hot spot is the warning of an impending blister. When you feel one coming on, stop immediately and cover it. Don't even consider trying to make it to the campsite first. Blisters take forever to heal when you are pounding on them every day for hours and will most likely become severe. If you take moleskin, you will need a small pair of scissors. Compeed, by Band-Aid, is a moleskin work-alike with medicine and comes in assorted sizes in a small container. The brand 2nd Skin is another option. Some swear by duct tape, but be careful. Duct tape and moleskin will remove a good chunk of meat if applied wrong or left too long, and leave you with worse wounds than when you began. Save the duct tape for equipment repairs. If you must use moleskin or duct tape, make sure that the offended part, i.e., the blister, has a barrier, like the cushion part of a Band-Aid.
- ***Insect repellent***: Jungle Juice is good. Just keep it away from eyebrows, as it tends to leave them smoldering. Some experienced hikers put a dab on the fingertip and touch it to the earlobes, which seems to work, strangely enough. Also recommended is Sawyer Controlled Release, or Broad Spectrum, for flying insects. Make sure whatever product you use has a little DEET in it, such as Off! Deep Woods (consult your pharmacist if you are unsure).
- *Sunscreen*: Sun protection lotion is a good addition to being mostly covered all the time. Put it on any exposed skin, especially face, neck and hands. And remember to wear your broad-brimmed hat. Even though the horse has left the barn of avoiding the sun a long time ago for us boomers, this is still good advice. Gadzooks, I remember slathering up in pure coconut oil sold in an old 12-ounce Coke bottle for a buck when I was in the Philippines, 20 years old, and not too smart about avoiding sun damage.
- *ChapStick*: With sun and wind exposure, lips tend to painfully

crack on the trail, so you'll want to protect them.
- *Gauze or feminine hygiene pads*: This is optional, but if you think you'll need to bandage something, they're great to use. You don't need to be squeamish about creative uses of special products; what works, works. Even Navy SEALs see them as part of a good pack in a combat zone.
- *Ace bandage*: Optional. An Ace can be used to wrap a sprained joint and help cover a bandaged wound.
- **Benadryl**: There is much that triggers allergies. Again, consult your physician when you get checked out for the trail. Some get sleepy with it, but when you are in the rigors of getting to the next camp, it doesn't seem to be a problem. Then again, you may wish to take a brief snooze after lunch.
- **Burn ointment**: Apply Neosporin for burns. Never bandage a burn unless it is third degree.
- **Rubbing alcohol (wintergreen)**: Believe it or not, this is another "don't leave home without it" item. It can be used for sterilizing hands after a walk in the woods behind the thunder tree. Wintergreen isopropyl rubbing alcohol foot massages are a great treat and practical, too, since it kills bacteria and eliminates odors from sweat. Moreover, these massages give you a chance to check out the old tootsies, since they are taking the biggest beating of any body part and are a major reason for getting knocked off the trail when they are diseased or injured.
- *Nail file*: Toenails need to be kept in check after the first week. You may want to splurge on weight and bring along a small nipper.

It will surprise you again how little you need by the way of supplies to keep the camp routine working well.

General Camp Equipment and Repairs

Good equipment, well-chosen and confidently used, is made for use in the outback. Care for your equipment the way you want it to take care of you. Don't be abusive, and your equipment will respond in kind.
- ***Pocketknife***: The Swiss Army Pioneer is all you need; I've been carrying one for more than 50 years. When you have one, you will

use it. This experience is not, nor should it become, a survival mission. Make sure the knife is sharp, and the awl blade, when stabbed with intent into a tree, can be used for a makeshift place from which to hang your hog-snout "shower." This method, however, should be used only when necessary; it's better to hang your shower from a tree limb, which is in keeping with the leave-no trace-philosophy.

- **Duct tape**: How did we ever emerge from the Dark Ages without duct tape? If you have it, there is no end to its uses: Temporarily patch your tent or sleeping bag, tape a flapping shoe sole to the shoe to make it serviceable till the next place to get new ones, fasten stuff together, etc. It is magical stuff in the outback, and it is easy to keep it wound around your water bottle ready for immediate use.
- **Light**: An LCD Petzl headlamp is just neat. It is tiny, it goes forever on small batteries, and it puts out a blazing light for its size, quite enough to settle in a dark tent or take a midnight stroll. You will put it on a time or two, even if you don't need it, just to look cool. Check your batteries *every* time you get ready for a hike. I personally like to read a bit before I nod off to the magical lullaby of the forest. Even as a light sleeper, I seem to sleep a bit better in the woods.

The next thing to be prepared for is personal hygiene. Just because you're out in the woods is no reason to skip brushing your teeth.

Toiletries and Toilet: There Is a Difference

Not much is needed here. I keep regular toiletries, toothpaste and soap in one baggie, and the TP and baby wipes in another, which is kept handy for the necessary trip. These can be replenished at the grocery store.

- **Toothpaste/brush/floss**: Surprisingly, on the trail you forget to use these things, but try to brush in the morning and before bed. Build it into your routine early on so it becomes habitual *before* you develop the habit of *not* doing it.
- **Personal soap**: Do something good for the environment and

make sure your soap is biodegradable. Try Dr. Bronner's or the like, which is shampoo and body wash all in one. Also, try your best to use detergents well away from streams. And if you're on a trail that encounters civilization now and again, doing a proper laundry by machine can wait for a hike into town or when spending a night at a hostel. Most clothes washing on the trail consists of rinsing out your wicking T-shirt, socks or underwear, which will be dry by morning. Again, freshly washed socks can be hung from the pack for a rather quick dry and a bit of disinfecting by the sun.

- *Camp soap*: This is mainly used to keep cooking utensils clean. There is nothing worse than bowel problems in the woods, which mainly come from unclean cooking utensils (or unpurified water).
- *Camp towel*: This is another not-so-trivial thing, and it dries in a flash when hung outside the pack, flapping next to that wet pair of socks and getting some air as you hike along.
- *Toilet paper*: This is for much more than the usual use. And no matter what they say, leaves just don't hack it. Take the good stuff, two ply. Take out the tube and crush the roll into a plastic zip-lock with the sterile wipes and/or your rubbing alcohol bottle. Cleanliness is one of the first things abandoned, and yet TP is one of the most needed items while being miles and sometimes a day or two from any assistance. Having TP and sanitized disposable cloths, or baby wipes, is especially important for the comfort of a hike.
- *Feminine hygiene products*: Everyone, female or male, must get used to necessities in the woods, and you get over it very quickly. Just be prepared to haul out non-biodegradable products. I repeat, even men should take a few, as they are good for first aid.
- *Alcohol wipes*: These are baby wipes, which are the best for the nether regions. Keep your hands sterile, especially after a nature break. Some folks take a very small bottle of liquid hand sanitizer also.
- *Comb*: Men are a bit luckier here, as a buzz cut negates the need for one. Women may like at least a non-breakable comb or brush.

Orienteering and Daily Journal Logging

As we've discussed before, a good habit to get into is knowing where you are, even if it is on a well-established trail. And a log can be as simple as notes on the map or guide. So why not take the next step and cultivate a habit of keeping a daily written record of what you are doing in a journal? Journaling is a personal thing. It has occurred to me that many of the most accomplished people journal. To me, writing things down is second nature. Take this book, for example; it is the result of taking notes throughout the process of getting back into nature, which began by dreaming of something neat to do—actually, a bucket list item. The act of writing is the beginning of doing. You are no longer wishing for something, it is happening. Acting makes all the difference between a life waiting for the perfect circumstance of time, money and opportunity to do the things that make a life worth living. A bucket list is just a bucket unless you dip into it regularly.

- *Maps*: Take only what you need for the scheduled hike. The U.S. Geological Survey has just about everything mapped. Obviously, new hikers need to stay on the beaten path until outdoors skills and confidence develop. Remember, an electronic device will lose battery power. The phone should be kept off to conserve power for the necessary call or location confirmation. National trails are well-documented, the AT being one of the most meticulously chronicled. Take only what is needed for the section you are hiking by simply copying those pages and keeping them in a plastic bag with the corresponding maps and notes. I hike with folks who take maps even for a walk on the local nature trails. They just like to always know where they are, which is a necessary habit to develop.
- *Compass*: Know how to use it and then do so, especially when you don't need it. It is too late to figure it out when you do. A compass works best when laid on a map so you can orient it to the map's direction, allowing you to more easily see your direction and position. It may also be helpful to glance toward the sun when you take that hourly break and mentally note direction and time. It becomes second nature. Orienteering can be used anywhere.

I remember seeing a couple on a street corner of Washington, DC, quite obviously lost. I merely asked for their map, turned it to match the roads on which they were standing, and they instantly could see how to get to where they were going. They thought I was guide guru, when all I did was apply one of the scores of valuable tools and practical bits of information I learned by saying yes to getting on the trail.

- *Orienting to time*: You will require at least a good hour or two to set up camp, eat and prepare for the next day, especially if you're tenting. We recommend more time for getting off your feet, just relaxing and doing nothing. Burt Kornegay of Slickrock Expeditions, friend and wilderness and canoeing guide extraordinaire, showed us a quick trick for telling time at the end of the day. A good way to know how much time you have, say, to get to and set up camp, is to extend your arm full length at a 90-degree angle to your body and then cock your fingers at a 90-degree angle to your arm. Rest your little finger on the horizon. Each finger width to the sun is 15 minutes. Try this a couple of times so you know what I am saying. Be in camp with at *least* four fingers to go. It is also good to allow two fingers of time for two fingers of a toddy and some conversation.
- *Journal and pen or pencil*: I do hope you journal. Regular paper journals don't cut it. Get a Rite in the Rain All-Weather Notebook from a college bookstore; it does quite well when wet. Accompany it with the smallest, best pen you can find. Again, now's the time to begin conditioning yourself to make regular writing a habit if you've a mind to. Most major personalities throughout history did it. Churchill commented that history would agree with him because he intended to write it; he did, and it still does. And he got the Nobel Prize for literature along the way.

And now, as Paul Harvey would say, it is time for "the rest of the story." There are always things that just defy organizing under a descriptive topic.

Miscellaneous

Another personal part of preparing for a hike is considering what is nice to have or do while you are alone and how to personalize your experience. For example, if you are a boomer, seriously consider taking hiking poles. With poles, you can put your arms and shoulders into your stride, which adds to how much you can hike in a day. Moreover, when you are competent with the poles, they add greatly to the safety factor. Four legs are better than two, especially going downhill.

- *Hiking poles and gloves*: You need a good pair of hiking poles. A single hiking stick is unbalanced and does not allow you to engage the upper body. This is a first-order piece of equipment, right up there with an excellent hiking partner and equally superior shoes. Don't go cheap! We suggest Leki trekking poles with titanium tips, which perform very well. Put them on properly by inserting your hands through the wrist strap from the bottom up, loosely enough that they swing as if on a hinge. Then adjust them so your arms are at a 90-degree angle to your body, with a firm grip on the handles and the tips firmly planted on the level ground. Make sure you use them—a lot—before the hike to get to know them. You should be able to use them properly and have a conversation at the same time, as you will be doing so on the trail. No kidding! The idea is to work with them until they become an unconscious extension of your body. Use them going up, down, and on the straight and level, where the proper grasp explained above will allow the poles to hinge forward to facilitate using your arms to help you walk. You will be able to hike much further, more safely and with less effort, especially going downhill over rocks. It will boost your hiking enjoyment factor significantly. Make sure you wear gloves, or you will suffer blisters. I have an ancient pair of pilot's gloves, but a pair of garden gloves with a rubber grip works well also.
- *Street clothes*: This is for the trip to and from the hike. Leave them in the locked and secured Hummer or Honda Insight, depending on your ecological driving statement.
- *Camp activities*: Take something like a book or parts of one that is too large to tote, games, sketch pad, cards, harmonica or your

first journal, just for starters. It's a good time to try something other than *Dancing with the Stars*. By the way, if the silliness of most TV does not strike you *before* the trip, let's hope it's struck a mortal blow after being without it, even for a little while. There is nothing real about a reality show, which is written to the lowest common denominator, and I suspect you are going on an outdoor experience because you are far from the media target audience. My apologies again for another digression.

- *Camera*: Take pictures, but only if you will put them in an album with commentary. Who knows who will be interested in your life path told in words, pictures and memorabilia, perhaps a grandchild? Experienced hikers have a digital point-and-shoot slung from a shoulder strap, ready for a near-instant snap. Naturally, use your mobile phone, but try to make a commitment to extract the best of the pictures to put in your photo journal. So many great pictures of life remain lost in some electronic folder, patiently waiting, never to be discovered. If you plan on taking pictures, read a photography book or go on the web for a little instruction before you go. Just a few hints and a little knowledge make a huge difference. Believe it or not, you do *not* need a smiling face in the center of every shot. And you can include many other things in an album besides pictures. How about that used piece of moleskin next to the picture of that Olympian blister from the new shoes you got for a song and didn't break in? I have sprigs of heather and gorse next to the pictures of them from the walk across England.
- *Money*: There will be expenses for gas, shuttle, parking, resupply, B&Bs at the hike launch and recovery sites, food to and from the trail, postage, a trip to the emergency room, a helicopter extraction out of wherever you are (cost is no deterrent), and extracurricular activities. Also, consider that some places don't do plastic. So, consider purchasing a belt that conceals a few bills and a credit card; your local outfitter should have a selection.
- *Wallet*: Experienced hikers weed out all the grocery discount cards; squirrels don't know how to use them. You only need a driver's license, credit card, phone numbers, some cash and maybe a

prepaid phone card—all of which can be put in a baggie and then in a zippered backpack pocket.

Ignore This Advice at Your Peril

This list is a result of classes, chats with other hikers, reading, thinking and trial-by-trail-miles on what may be needed or at least considered. Suggested items are a trade-off between what can be taken and consideration for weight. Yet there are personal decisions and choices about what is essential. That is, some may argue about the need for a stove, but the well-equipped boomer like me *will* have hot beverages and meals. And some folks say a tarp or a hammock will do instead of a tent . . . not. There is *one* rule for the sum of your gear:

> **Goal: 30 to 35 pounds *with* food and water!**
> **The trail will make a believer of you.**
> **Heed or suffer!**

If you haven't hiked before, you will ignore this advice . . . once. You will get all sorts of advice on what to take, but the best advice is to pack light, even ultralight, as much as possible. One of the main reasons for quitting a wonderful hike is taking too much weight, which discourages even the college athlete or takes you away from a view that took a lifetime to get to because of a sprained wrist caused by falling from ungainly weight wrongly packed. Did I say that you will fall? You will. So, minimize the chances of a big fall and impact with a strategically placed hunk of granite or branch. You can bet you won't fall on something soft; it is just not in Mother Nature's rules. If we can't convince you now, the first "little" hill will. This means forget the pound of honey, even if it is in a "light" plastic jar, and the flagon of Chianti, even if it is in the platypus (oh, yes, people do this).

Another point about conserving weight: No weight savings is too trivial. Even removing all but one credit card from your wallet makes a difference, and that's if you even take a wallet. You think we jest? Trade your bear-bag carabiner for a small cloth bag you can fill with stones. Rip the pocket book of Gibbon's *Decline and Fall of the Roman Empire* into sections that match the sections of the hike. Look for the smallest and most reliable journaling pen you can find. Always experiment with weight reduction; it all adds up. And it is so satisfying to get the pack below the magic 35 pounds and still be comfy, confident, cozy, equipped and safe.

CHAPTER 8
Food

*It is not so much for its beauty that the forest
makes a claim upon men's hearts, as for that subtle
something, that quality of the air, that emanation
from the old trees, that so wonderfully changes
and renews a weary spirit.*
—Robert Louis Stevenson

*Crackerjack with English bangers and mash in
stout gravy—the smile says it all*

Some say that the success of the trip rests on food, but experienced distance hikers are casual about food if there is a way to take frequent and simple nutrition and water breaks. Decisions about trail food and hydration are made by the weight and nutrition of each item, in that order. Nearly every item is unpackaged if it should be, smashed if it can be, repackaged in much smaller condition and reassembled into complete meals. For example, a breakfast plastic baggie can contain cereal, powdered milk, a little dried fruit and sugar; all you need to add is water, and heat is optional. I've seen some hikers put the water in their breakfast baggie the night before to have it palatable by morning and to save heating it. There is so much creativity to a hike, which adds to the experience and the *fun*.

Food is a very personal thing. What you take depends on so many factors. Once you see what others eat, you will be pleasantly surprised at how simple adequate fare is. Finally, you won't care much about the sauce and presentation of your cuisine when the last eight hours cost you 5,000 calories, give or take, and your belly is so slack it's flapping. You will remember those simple meals warmed on your cup-sized stove much more than the ones served on linen by liveried staff, and *that* is the point.

A Matter of Perspective

That being the case, we will dole out our advice from the perspective of a hiker anticipating more than one night on the trail and on some quite rugged terrain, meaning lots of ups and downs and at least eight hours per day putting leather on the trail. To be sure, if it is edible, someone has tried and certainly considered how to haul it with the means to prepare it. You will find that you don't need much and you certainly don't need fancy. Just stay fueled and hydrated; don't obsess over details and enjoy what you got off the beaten path for anyway, like getting into your tent just after 6 p.m. because the sun is going behind the mountain and you don't have anything else to do, and, better yet, there is no one who is going to argue about it. You should have a cozy night's sleep, in sync with sunrise and sunset.

The following sustained one distance-wilderness hiker for about three days on a national mountainous trail. It was all that was needed and was easy to replenish along the way:

Three packages of Pop-Tarts, eight Nutri-Grain bars, six to eight energy bars (Clif Energy Bars, PowerBar, PowerBar Harvest and perhaps Snickers[13]), three packs of crackers, two boxes of Kraft Mac &

---

13 While many hikers swear by candy bars, be aware of their effect on the body. You get an initial energy rush, but then you may quickly become sluggish. The lesson here is to be aware of good carbohydrates, such as those in pasta, which arguably give you better and more sustained energy.

Cheese, three Knorr noodles and sauce envelopes, one freeze-dried dinner, potato flakes, various snacks (usually two to three per day of candy bars, oatmeal creme pies, yogurt mix, etc.), and coffee.

These provisions are high-carb and high-calorie, just what is needed. Little of it needs to be cooked. It can be eaten with little or no preparation, even on the fly, and it can be replenished anywhere—plus it's all pretty tasty, especially when driven by the need for calories and deep breathing pure air. What this menu demonstrates is that eating on the trail is as individual as the hiker and not complicated.

Menu Planning

Lay out your daily meals on a spreadsheet (like the simple one below); at the very least, it makes a good shopping list. And a word to the wise: Try the diet before you do the actual hike. Some foods individually or in a new combination may simply not agree with you. You may want more variety because some food becomes monotonous. Some foods may just take too long to prepare and still taste like cardboard. Just as an aside, when certain long-distance hiking milestones are reached, hikers, even the most petite women, have been known to celebrate with a *gallon* of ice cream.

DAY	Breakfast	#	Snack	#	Lunch	#	Snack	#	Dinner	#
				HIKER'S MENU PLANNER						
1										
2										
3										
4										
5										
6										
Totals										

When filling in this chart, list the food items you will have for the meal. Also, note how many of each one you need. This becomes your shopping list and will aid your packing, as some items you may wish to build. For example, you may want to prepare an all-in-one breakfast baggie of hot cereal, dried fruit, hemp seeds, sugar and powdered milk—all ready for water and your little alcohol stove.

Be sensible: Eat five to six times per day, consisting of three main meals and snacks between, which are a great excuse for a pack-off break. A hiker is constantly occupied, either in motion or with the activities of being on the trail, so fuel for the body must be equally constant.

Meals don't have to be big, either. Strawberry fluff (marshmallow) on a bagel for breakfast with coffee is mercifully simple and quick, and will sustain you till your midmorning snack. For lunch, you might have soup (if you care to cook at lunch), cheese (don't take soft cheeses, which will melt in heat), and sausage or hard salami with a few crackers. Supper should take a little time. Pasta and cheese with some bagged meat and something for dessert is easy and filling. It is nice to snack between these three main meals without a care about calories.

This is exactly what all those designer diets want you to understand: It doesn't matter what you eat if it is sensible, moderate and balanced, and is combined with exercise. What better way to learn these lessons than by doing just that surrounded by pristine nature? And enjoy, because you will rarely have a better opportunity to get in such good shape—body, mind and soul.

Convenient But Nutritious

There is another important point to be made here about proper nutrition at any time, let alone for some of the best, most rigorous exercise you will get. Hikers, especially distance hikers—the folks who spend more than a week and 50 miles on the trail—lean toward convenience; they must. However, we do not advocate Pop-Tarting your way through a hike. Instead, spend some time learning how to put together an interesting and wholesome diet for your trip.

Hopefully the items discussed below will help you arrive at what is right for you.

Again, the experienced hiker adapts to what the local grocer has and keeps it in the plastic grocery bag; a stuff sack weighs too much. Three days' provisions are plenty for most trails; maybe pack for a day more for peace of mind. While the discussion is on a longer hike of a week or more, we are aware that most hikes may be a weekender or a few days, so provisioning isn't a consideration. But by discussing the longer hike, the hiker doing a shorter one will be well-prepared; it is a confidence builder. Take heart that many hikers get by on very little, even on a diet that may seem a little bereft.

Take Poco Loco, whom we met on a mountaintop when he came to our camp and took over the shelter (he had no tent). It was obvious he knew what to do, as evidenced by his many hiking tales. And he looked like a hiker: lean, small pack, a humble air of confidence, a broad step, and efficient camp processes. Poco Loco sat down to his evening's repast after his usual 16-mile day on the AT, pulled out his plastic grocery bag, and dined on grapefruit, a bologna sandwich and a candy bar, because, "That is what they had in the local minimart." He was also the first in his sleeping bag at night and the first out of camp in the morning, fed, rested and fit, if not punctured by a few terrorist mosquitoes as he slept on a ground cover in the lean-to shelter. He had hiked all over Arizona and a few major trails on both coasts. He was well over 65 years old and could walk the boots off most folks half his age.

Keeping Fueled From "Me" and "You"

Me and You, the trail names of a neat couple who had a lot of fun with their trail names, were well on their way to thru-hiking the AT when we met them. We spent a wonderful evening with them in an old barn overlooking one of God's very green acres in the Tennessee Smokies. We got to talking food. They were well-fed, lean, full of pep and could walk the hooves off a pack mule. Me was all of 116 pounds, at about 5 feet 4 inches in her mountaineering boots. While this is a more thorough list of what to bring, it is useful to know what people arrive at for food after a remarkable hike and several months in the woods. Here is some of what they recommended for keeping fueled on the trail:

Eating Equipment
- *Cookpot*: Get titanium. It is way too expensive, but it is a bite-the-bullet-anyway item. It is light, serviceable and indestructible. You will be using it two or three times a day, and with any luck on many subsequent trips. Naturally, it needs to be big enough to contain your stove, which will handily boil 16 ounces of water and an evening meal.
- *Fry pan and lid*: Titanium again.
- *Stove and windscreen*: The little Trangia stove and pot system seems to work well, but you will get many opinions. You will need a small aluminum windscreen if you do any amount of cooking, which will help conserve fuel. A slight breeze cuts efficiency way, way down. The windscreen is a fiddly thing, but you usually have time to fiddle if blueberry muffins are at stake. Again, make sure it nestles in the cookpot with your lighter and perhaps your spoon or spork as well.
- *Cooking utensils*: A plastic spatula is plenty good; cut the handle to fit in the fry pan for storage.
- *Fuel*: A nearly full sports bottle of denatured alcohol is all that should be packed. It can usually be purchased at the local minimart. If the weather is warm and calm, and you only heat coffee, tea, or an instant breakfast meal in the morning and one meal in the evening, a sports bottle of fuel can last a week or more. But when the temperature dips into the 40s and there is a breeze, even the tiny Trangia sucks fuel like a blowtorch.
- *Camp suds*: Be meticulous and methodical about hygiene. Wash your eating equipment well. Any kind of gastrointestinal problem is simple to avoid, and if encountered, impossibly complicated in the boonies. There is no greater adventure than sphincter-challenging sprints for even a few yards.

- *Camp towel or small sponge*: You will use this morning and night, religiously. Your towel is for your morning or evening shower. Your sponge is used for cleaning the cookpot and squeegeeing rain or dew off the tent.
- *Nalgene container*: This is about a 16-ounce, airtight, screw-on lid container, which is used to rehydrate the next meal while you hike. Having supper slosh around for 10 hours cuts down the cooking time while opening many more gastronomic possibilities. How clever is that!
- *Food stuff sack*: Again, all Me and You had was a single plastic grocery bag, which most grocers are happy to replace, brand-spanking-new, free of charge, such a deal. Many times you can even get a double bag without asking.

Meals
Breakfast
- *Coffee*: Most hikers just don't give up their brew. Luckily, single-serving coffee bags, like tea bags, are passable for a jolt of beloved caffeine, which when used remain in a neat, biodegradable sachet, ready to pack out or bury. And for a real treat, regular ground coffee dumped directly in a screaming pot of boiling water makes great camp brew. It never ceases to amaze more than a few travelers that the grounds sink to the bottom at just the right time and temperature for a sincerely good morning cup. And, oh, what a smell in the morning! Please don't try instant, if only for the fact you may be camping with a coffee lover.
- *Cereal with dried milk*: Breakfast should be premeasured into separate baggies; note speed and efficiency here. Or . . .
- *A granola bar*: This is instead of cereal if the mood strikes, or if you want a no-cook, speedy departure from camp in the morning.
- *Snacks, Clif Bar*: These seem to stay edible forever, and they are tolerably tasty, since they come in an appealing array of popular flavors.

Lunch
- *Peanut butter and flour tortilla roll-ups,* or . . .
- *Dehydrated mac and cheese with summer sausage or other hard salami*

Dinner
- *Rice*: Uncle Ben's, or . . .
- *Pasta,* and . . .
- *Packaged meat, such as chicken or fish*: Consider adding these meats to meals such as ramen noodles, which don't require extensive cleanup.
- *Dessert*: Muffin mix in your covered fry pan doesn't look pretty, but hot and steamy off the trail stove, it is a French hillside culinary delight.
- *Other food to make the meal and keep up calories*: Isn't hiking grand? Go ahead, eat a half gallon of handmade ice cream at the next town; I dare you. Make a memory.
- *Olive oil*: About a 4-ounce bottle.
- *Seasonings*: Flavorings to taste, in small (pill) bottles. (Zatarain's is amazing stuff.)

If you regularly take vitamins, don't stop. Have your daily doses individually wrapped in a Kleenex and keep them in a plastic baggie, for example. If you need a prescription or two, treat them the same way as vitamins.

For the most part, this list is as complete and as light as possible, yet there are many ways to get lighter.

Personalize It: Your Pack Is Yours

The bottom line is that your pack and your hike are yours. Add and subtract as you see fit, but make your own list. This basic list serves several purposes. From it, you can make a few additions and deletions to reflect different experiences; for example, to pack winter hiking equipment and food checklists, or checklists for hiking from town to town or day packing from B&B to B&B. Most important, a checklist serves as a surefire way to remember what makes your hike complete, safe and comfortable because you are confident in your preparation and feel certain nothing is left out. Your learning curve on your first trip will be off the charts; planning and packing for the next trip will be reduced to hours rather than weeks or months. For example, I keep my first aid, toilet and personal grooming baggies packed and ready to go in my day pack. No packing necessary. I am ready to go on a day hike, fishing or running German Shorthair Pointers in Montana on a whim.

Stewball, a seasoned hiker we met at the outfitter in Hot Springs, North Carolina, located on the AT, advises, "Stay warm, stay fed, stay hydrated, enjoy." He did the whole 2,180-plus miles[14], give or take a few miles, food and all, with a 20-pound pack! And let me tell you, when you are prepared, knowledgeable, trail-hardened, lean and mean, hostile, agile, and mobile, you will feel as if you can fly with that kind of experience, confidence and especially minimal weight. Plus, the enjoyment factor goes way up. But before we continue preparation for hitting the trail, let's resume the C2C hike midway from Shap to Kirkby Stephen.

---

14 Actually, the trail changes slightly from year to year as trail managers, maintainers and an army of volunteers add to, reroute or shorten it.

Frank's Bridge and residents of Kirkby Stephen who will gladly take any crumbs offered

STAGE 6: SHAP TO KIRKBY STEPHEN

Chris and Wes decided to take the bus to Kirkby Stephen, which was standard operating procedure when you wished to have a day of zero hiking and still stay on schedule with your prearranged B&B reservations. I went on alone and really missed their company. In fact, I contemplated turning back for the bus. Thank goodness, I caught up to Stephen and Liz from Arizona within the first mile. It was great to have hiking partners—and even better that they turned out to be quite vigorous and experienced ones. You could see it in their step, pace, and cheerful, comfortable mood on the trail. Their division of labor had been worked out on trails all over the world: Stephen navigated from the Stedman book, second in line to Liz, who set a jaunty pace (meaning I dare you to keep up) in front. I also like a good pace if your body and all your equipment are functioning. Even though grandmothers do this hike, the guidebooks talk about nasty blisters and various pains at this stage of the hike, which is just over a third of the way through.

Food

"Steveo" had tucked the Stedman book over his belt front for instant reference. Liz stayed in the lead the whole way and was seemingly casual until you tried to keep up. Her pace was at least 3.5 mph, which is stepping out smartly when the day holds 20-plus miles. Steve read the narrative directions and commentary nearly every step of the way.

We had most enjoyable conversations about everything. Liz is a professor of communications and was publishing another book for a large publishing house. She also helped me with my forthcoming presentation in Fort Worth, Texas. The day passed most pleasantly.

A 20-mile-plus day is tough, even though the day pack was a merciful 15 pounds or so. After even a few miles, it was still a burden. I remember taking it off at the end of one day, and I got the sensation I was floating over the ground.

On this day I got lucky. No less than 100 yards from the Old Coach House B&B, my left knee began to make noise. By the time I found the B&B, I was in pain. Fortunately, I was in store for a real treat, one of the best meals on the whole trail. Wes and Chris met me with a spread of two wines, two cheeses, fruit, smoked mackerel and bread. No repast can be better—friends, fatigue, failing body parts, food and fabulous wine at the end of a picturesque, glorious day.

New memories were made nearly every step of the way. There is a picture in my "England" album with my wind-reddened face, a bit of a blank stare and bread in my hand. It felt good to be alive, and such pleasures can be had by any man or woman. All you need to do is scoop them up.

Wes wanted to have a birthday drink; he turned 24 that day. So we each had a small shot of really good scotch as we leaned on a stone fence, chatting, watching the sun set and the sheep settle in for the night. It can't get better than that.

PART IV: HITTING THE TRAIL

Today is your day! Your mountain is waiting.
So . . . get on your way!
—Dr. Seuss

Coming into Kirkby Stephen

The moment has finally arrived—you're ready to hit the trail. This part of *The Honest Backpacker* ties up a few loose ends you may want to consider, some things to make the hike just a little better. The wisdom is dispensed in two chapters: Culled from personal experience and seasoned hikers, Chapter 9, "Trail-Tested Wisdom from The Honest Backpacker," lists additional advice to help get you ready. The wisdom in Chapter 10, "Correcting Errata," comes from Ben Franklin, who was inspired by nature and the realization that if we are blessed with growing old, we have a responsibility to do a little better, give back and perhaps correct a few things. Ben was right when he helped found this Republic—and he is right now.

CHAPTER 9
Trail-Tested Wisdom from The Honest Backpacker

For after all, the best thing one can do when it is raining, is to let it rain.
—Henry Wadsworth Longfellow

The last few moments on the Coast-to-Coast

I don't want to diminish the need for a plan. Planning is paramount. The comprehensiveness and work you put into planning is in direct correlation to the success of your endeavor. It is the definition of foolishness to begin such a demanding feat without planning. But it can't be ironclad: You can't plan meticulously, endlessly looking for every fact and overturning every rock to be 100 percent ready. If you follow *The Honest Backpacker*, you will be ready and confident. So, set a departure date, where the planning ends and the doing starts—and stick to it.

The following tips are activities you might want to do on the eve of departure, as well as a few miscellaneous ones that didn't fit anywhere else in the book yet are nice to consider. They come from the school of "I told you so," which everyone attends on the trail. Part of the purpose of *The Honest Backpacker* is to keep you from making easily avoidable mistakes. The goal is to limit your mistakes to novel ones you may invent just for the fun of it, like the types that begin with, "Hey, hold my beer and watch this."

Tip 1: Stop and Smell the Jasmine
Once you begin putting shoe leather on the trail, do everything possible to have a good time and make it memorable, even if it means making a 3-mile day instead of a 10-miler. If you like the luxury of a pillow rather than a stuff sack full of last week's socks and T-shirts, take it. If the whim strikes to head to town for a pizza rather than eating tired ol' ramen yet again, do it. If someone suggests staying in a particular place for an extra day, and it seems reasonable, do it. If it looks like the weather is closing in and the hostel is just a little farther, take a chance and hike on. If you feel a hamstring starting to whisper to you, take a break. The point is to organize the amount and detail of preparation that gets you on the trail with measured confidence, reasonably competent in the tasks of the trail, and back again safely. Take the time to smell the air filled with jasmine.

Experienced hikers get that the trail dictates the hike somewhat. One of the most charming and endearing sights we came upon was a lone hiker on a mountaintop, slung between two trees on her hammock in silk running shorts and a sports bra, making notes in her journal—the picture of contentment. She had just hiked an 18-mile mountainous day the day before, through some of the more demanding portions of the AT, and thought a little break would be nice. So, she stopped to capture on paper what Ansel Adams tried to capture with a snapshot. No picture really grasps what there is to see with the naked eye. By-the-by, she was a 65-year-old retired schoolteacher. Excaver, I think she called herself. She gets it.

Tip 2: Check Hiking Conditions Around Start Time
Note that there are various "classes" of hikes determined by the hiking conditions, just as there are classes of rivers to canoe or kayak

and various mountains to scale. The type of hike you anticipate determines the information and skills you will need. I found out about fabulous canoe trips down magical rivers and took a canoeing basics class over a weekend with an outfitter to learn all the background, theory and skills of canoeing, then practiced them on a very still and flat lake. Afterward, I was ready for Class III rapids.

Tip 3: Assemble Gear
Again, inventory what you have and only buy essentials. It is easy to go overboard. Remember, experienced hikers do the AT with only a 20-pound pack by sleeping in shelters, eating cold food, leaving the stove at home and shopping at convenience stores along the route (see Chapter 7, "Gear"). Then again, other outdoor adventures will be totally remote, like the canoe trips I took down the Rio Grande and the Grand Ronde rivers. The outfitter planned for everything; every one of the seven canoes was packed full of gear. He even brought good whisky and cigars to celebrate the first riverside encampment and a roaring fire as all became dear friends.

I realize many of you will want to do remote hikes where provisioning along the route will be difficult. To state the obvious, there needs to be a little more planning to have certain daily hiking goals, provisions along the way to the next stop, and a little cushion to ensure you make it to the resupply points. The opposite is true for that impromptu day hike, where only a day pack, a snack, a toilet kit and water are needed. Naturally, your hiking outfit, good boots, broad-brimmed hat and hiking poles with gloves are always at the ready. Hiking is very much a question of common sense, taught by the trail and combined with the knowledge and skills base of the individual hiker.

Tip 4: Plan Transportation To and From the Hike
We began our AT small-section hike in Damascus, Virginia, and headed south as recommended for novice, boomer AT hikers such as ourselves. You may want to follow suit and consider beginning your hike at a trailhead chosen for its great side activities, even if it is just a good chicken-fried steak, as can only be made in the mountains.

Damascus, for example, offers the Virginia Creeper Trail (50 downhill miles on an old logging railroad bed; rent a bike and do it, stopping for ice cream halfway down), the Damascus Old Mill Restaurant, and celebrations galore for Trail Days[15], which happens every year in May. Participating in the hoedown at the barn dance hall Saturday night is compulsory.

- *Rendezvous the day of the trip.* The fun begins. Did I say that this is all about having fun, making friends and creating memories? Somehow even the worst jokes make people laugh, so bring a bunch of them, or at least don't be embarrassed to let a few fly. Yes, hiking is rough business, but you will never laugh anywhere else like you will on the trail. Funny stuff happens, like meeting "Fantasy Feet," his trail name, in the middle of the Great Smoky Mountains, a charming fellow who may have made one too many trips to Haight-Ashbury in San Francisco in the '60s. He extolled the virtue of his umbrella, his only raingear, which he slung from his shoulder strap "in case it rains." We were reminded of Mary Poppins floating down the trail, which was good for more than a few miles of jokes. Pause for a moment and imagine that. Sometimes laughter is the only thing to do, as all other responses to trail reality or stupidity just don't cut it. Don't worry, you will do stupid stuff too, so get used to it; laugh because you will be laughed with (or at).
- *Travel to the trailhead.*
    - *Spend your last night in comfort*: Treat yourself to a good B&B the night before if there is one near the trailhead (if not, spend the night at the trailhead). Linger in the morning shower and pile on the pancakes, eggs, ham, biscuits, gravy, and coffee with cream and honey without guilt. Or keep with that sensible diet of reasonable proportions—your choice.
    - *Park your car for the duration*: Make sure your vehicle is safely parked and out of the way, gassed and ready for the return trip. Parking at the B&B is another plus to starting from one, as your vehicle will be relatively secure and mostly under a watchful eye.

---

15 http://traildays.us/index.php?id=12. If you go, make sure you stay at the Lazy Fox Inn and be enchanted by the proprietress, Ginny Adams. Have some apple butter seasoned with Red Hots candy—sublime.

Parking at some trailheads is not secure, even though your vehicle may be in a crowded parking lot. Some B&Bs or nearby outfitters will shuttle you back to your vehicle by prearrangement and a call when you are ready.
- *Return to trailhead.* Make sure you arrange for any return transportation, usually an established shuttle.
- *Return home.* You will be beat and ready for your own bed, but that will come later. For now, plan on a relaxing drive home from the trailhead or the campsite. And there's nothing like loading '60s rock 'n' roll on the CD player, rolling the windows down, and pretending you know the words to "Riders on the Storm"[16] or claiming you are the only one who knew what the heck Bob Dylan was really trying to say. I guarantee that by this time, you can get away with just about anything with your trail mates. Everything is fodder for a thoughtful moment or a belly-rolling laugh. This is therapy we all need. The stressors of our lives lie ahead. But on the trip home, they don't matter.

Tip 5: Get the Most Out of Your Hike
- *Review any trail guides for your hike.* It is always a good practice to know where you are going, where you are and how you will get back. Constant orienteering is like flying: A pilot is constantly making sure he is on the flight plan. The idea is to know almost instantly when you may be veering off-course, so you can correct before you need to backtrack. Or, worse yet, must descend to a river and follow it to a road or civilization, which is a kind of last-ditch fix to being lost. You will be disoriented even on the most traveled trails. Many a fork in the road will be wrongly taken. Be aware.
- *Set daily mileage goals.* Plan and act according to your performance on the trail. The first week will be one of the toughest. Again, no matter how good you are, take it easy. Some say that the first few days should be only a few miles per day, and it can take a few weeks to become trail-hardened, even if you consider yourself in shape.

---
[16] If you must ask who sang "Riders on the Storm," you are too young to be reading this book. Hint: It has something to do with the entry portal to a house.

You are the judge. Whatever your goal, build in time to stop, relax, smell your ripe T-shirt and enjoy the quiet of nature. Leave plenty of time to make camp, including finding good water, and to break camp after a decent breakfast and "leave no trace" scouting mission.

- *Set a hiking pace and routine.* Set your pace with the appropriate point man. This should *not* be your fastest, ablest, happiest wanderer. Doing an average of 2 miles per hour is a goodly accomplishment. This clip includes breaks and lunch. Look to do an average of 10 miles per day after you are trail-hardened and have a routine, which includes making/breaking camp and other stops. You will find that is a respectable pace. Forget the stories of 30-mile days; those people may take some down time or a "zero" day to recover, so the average is still 10 miles per day. Chat up anyone coming in the opposite direction for conditions, water, campsites, peculiarities, and the inevitable neat tidbits about life coming your direction on the trail.
- *Choose appropriate campsites.* The preferred site has at least the following characteristics: good and reliable water within a half mile of camp and a relatively flat tent site that's elevated from running rain, free from pointy rocks just below the grass cover, and not exposed to either wind or stuff that can be naturally pruned from trees in the night (for example, rotten tree limbs) or roll downhill. Weather permitting, ditch the tent and sleep under the stars; there really is something to that experience that hasn't quite been bred out of us since we first set foot on terra firma. And the air is the best you will ever breathe.
- *Select quality water sites.* Look for running water, and remember to purify, no matter how good the water looks and tastes. Even the best-looking, crisp, clear, cool water can be chock-full of disease-bearing microbes that have knocked many a hiker off the trail, permanently. Purify at the water source, every time. A couple of drops of SweetWater, or any recommended water sterilizer, will do it. Don't drink it for at least 20 minutes, and then enjoy. Experienced hikers simply use two drops of a scent-free Clorox per liter from a small Visine eye-drops bottle. This saves a few ounces, and weight is

everything after the first mile. You laugh at saving even this amount of weight, but you will see.
- *Take time for rest breaks.* Frequent, at least hourly, rest is a good thing; so is lunch. Take pack-on and pack-off breaks. Even a slight incline may cause you to lean on your hiking sticks and breathe deeply for a few minutes or so. That's called a pack-on break. Every hour, take the pack off for a few minutes and drink! You will forget to drink—don't. Remember to drink water, even in cool weather. Time hydrating to the hourly rest stops, or more frequently. Pace yourself slowly. Mileage really does not matter. Health and lasting to the next day do; make sure that sinks in. Also remember to keep on a regular eating schedule, even when—again, not if—your appetite disappears.
- *Don't forget the side trips.* It pays to stop and contemplate things. You will pass many sites of interest, either curious, historical, natural, biological or downright astounding. Don't pass up a chance to take a dip in anything larger than a puddle, if only to experience trout water that numbs the toes before you have the courage to splash your face. Resupply often, say, every few days if the trail allows it, because it keeps the pack light and you meet all sorts of interesting folks in that bend in the road called a town. To reiterate, if you do a rather remote hike, plan food to last between resupply stops and a little extra in case you need to spend a little more time getting to the next resupply point, which may be as simple as a convenience store at a gas station. In extreme hiking, which is rare, someone can meet you at a way station with supplies or they can be sent ahead. This need for frequent resupplying implies an intimate, daily knowledge of the trail map so you know the crossroads that lead to facilities, food and services. (Refer to Tip 6 on page 139.)
- *Adjust your gear, if necessary.* Adjust anything that is bumping, grinding, chafing or even thinking about doing any of these. It only takes once for you to ignore this advice, and you'll never do it again. A hot spot can turn bloody without your knowledge, and that is problematic on a mountaintop when the hike must proceed, pain or no pain.

- *Remember, it's not a race.* Put the sprinter in the middle or the end of your group, if that person wants to stay with the group. Just don't let the fastest person set the pace. You only need to go as fast as the slowest person in line. This keeps morale up and lessens the chances of leaving someone behind. It's safer, too. Find out who the morning person is and put him or her on sweep. If that person is pooped in the afternoon, *then* he or she can lead. A moderate pace also lessens the chance of injury and certainly provides more opportunity to observe anything you want. One other thing: Leave a decent few paces or more between hikers. If you are too close, the chance of getting hit by a branch whipped by the hiker ahead is great. Those branches are usually head-high, too. Go downhill too close together, and you could fall into the person ahead of you, and vice versa. And some people just don't like someone breathing down their necks.
- *Appoint a leader and a backup leader.* Someone should be in charge, especially of larger or inexperienced groups. Even though the majority are easily made communal decisions, someone needs to make the executive decisions.
- *Review each day's hike over breakfast.* Discuss things like water locations, direction, landmarks, timetable, weather predictions, orientation by sun and clock, bailout sites (for example, when someone in your party must leave the hike, usually for some injury), sightseeing, etc.
- *Know where you are.* Most established trails like the AT are so well-marked that you become quickly complacent about remaining aware of where you are. It is so easy to take the proverbial fork in the road the *wrong* way. Always know where you are. You're never lost if you can backtrack to a familiar spot, so continually note landmarks such as ridgelines, outcrops and stream crossings, and look behind you so you'll recognize them on the way back if you are doing an out-and-back hike.

  Take a hint from adventure racers: Never pack away your map. Keep it handy in a breast pocket or folded over your waistband so you can refer to it often, even on well-trodden and marked trails where wandering off the trail is easy to do. Stay oriented by frequently comparing the actual and the virtual terrain. This is not difficult. Do it until it becomes second nature.

Orient with a compass, and make it a routine early on. All it takes is getting lost on the trail one time, and you will eagerly preview each day. One time when I was double-timing it down a narrow path from one of the peaks in Zion National Park, I took a few steps to the left on what looked like the trail, but it wasn't. Rather, it led to a sheer drop of 1,000 feet! I obviously lived to tell the tale, but it's a good lesson as to why you should be intimate with the trail beforehand. My heart still pounds for a beat or two at the thought of Zion.

- *Have a plan if you get lost.* This shouldn't happen on established trails, but if you want to be completely prepared, there are many books about wilderness survival. Also, there are a few common-sense things to keep in mind if this rarity should happen. If you get lost and feel the need to move, go up to a place where you can see more of where you are. By nature, humans tend to travel down when lost; that is wrong. You need to get a fix on your position. The sun always rises in the east. Figure out where you are and proceed from there. If worse comes to worst, follow a river downstream; it usually leads to some civilization. You may want to carry detailed maps, a rescue whistle, a solar-operated communication device or a personal GPS on unfamiliar excursions. If you miss a trail marking, such as the famous white blazes on the AT, even for a *few feet,* you are off the trail. Just retrace your steps immediately. Stay together, or at least don't lose sight of each other. And solo hikers should exercise just a little more caution and wariness about staying located.

Tip 6: Bone Up on Trail Nutrition

If you need to control your diet and get in the habit of exercising, hiking is *the* way to do it. You will get in shape and perhaps learn a different lifestyle to keep you in shape for the rest of your days. Many people find these experiences life-changing. (See Chapter 8, "Food," for menu planning.)

- *Eat regularly.* You won't want to eat much early on. Eat anyway. You will be burning about 400 to 500 calories per hour beyond your individual maintenance calories with your pack on depending on terrain, so it is important to eat (and hydrate) frequently.
- *Decide which meals you will cook on the trail, and which you won't.* To cook or not to cook, that is *really* the question. Experienced hikers cook at least a simple supper, such as seasoned pasta and some packaged meat with a dessert. However, there are several reasons for cooking breakfast as well. A hot meal is good for morale, and it jump-starts the day. But there is also a practical rationale for cooking breakfast: The process of heating begins to break down the food prior to digestion, allowing you to gain energy from that food quicker. It takes more calories to digest raw, uncooked or cold food than it does hot. The same goes for consuming warm water, especially green tea (which is just a bit better for you than perhaps black tea or coffee).
- *Plan a daily menu.* Pack just a little extra, depending on how long you want to stay on the trail. Besides water, food is your heaviest item, so keep it light; you usually only need a few days' supply on most trails. Weight is *everything*, and food is a controllable weight. If you are new to packing, you will ignore this advice and overpack . . . once. Whatever you do, make sure you try everything out first before you take it on the trail. For instance, while granola may be popular, it may be a bit much for the digestive system, especially when eaten every morning.
- *Handle your food carefully.* Eat at least five times per day, even though some "meals" are snacks by comparison. As stated earlier, you probably won't feel like eating early on in a hike of a week or more, but prepare to eat and do it. Be sanitary, for obvious reasons. Try to boil or scald eating utensils and dinnerware. Storing food carefully and using cleanliness with anything that is or smells like it is edible is mandatory. Sanitation for eating is obviously required, but it also keeps the critters somewhat at bay. Mice are fearless and prefer an expensive backpack as an appetizer on their way to a peanut entrée they *know* is somewhere in your pack.

- *Resupply food along the way.* Note that this tip only applies to long-distance hiking, not a trek that is a week or less. When you follow the planning timeline above, you will be aware of and assured of places to stop to resupply, which are usually conveniently just off trail a little way. A trip to town is an adventure. Hope you are whisked into town by a pickup, as a summer breeze is luxurious if you are lucky enough to ride in the truck bed, which brings back volumes of childhood memories for me.

Tip 7: Learn to Set Up and Break Camp Efficiently

Practice the philosophy of leave no trace, which simply means "if you pack it in, pack it out." It's easy to build this responsible philosophy into your routine. Build fires only if local conditions allow and are appropriate. I have been on some life-changing and life-affirming canoeing trips where *everything* was thrown into the fire. The fire took care of nearly everything, including incinerating aluminum cans. All that remained were tin cans, which we smashed and packed up in a small plastic bag. The refuse from 13 people and five days and four nights on the Rio Grande fit into one small bag, including the "honey bucket,"[17] which we leavened with cedar chips. There was very little evidence of our passing through, except perhaps flattened grass where the tents were.

- *Setting up camp*: Making camp always takes longer than you think, but there are ways to make it easier and even luxurious. Hang a "pig snout" bladder (one that has a valve that looks reminiscent of a pig's nose) for a shower. I stabbed my pocketknife in a tree at shower height and hung my bladder from that. Even just washing your face at night is a great refresher. Hammocks are becoming popular, especially for the distance hiker, though they take some getting used to, as they are persnickety to set up and demand the right two trees from which to hang. It's a good idea to have everything set up, dinner done, water replenished and purified for breakfast, and all preparations ready for the sack before sundown and an early turn-in. When you are in your groove, plan on doing about 8 to 10

---

17 Human waste

hours of hiking per day. This allows time for all making and breaking camp duties.

- *Breaking camp*: Plan on an early but comfortable start. Prepare for breaking camp the night before. Make sure you have plenty of water for breakfast and the morning's hike or to the next good water source. Set out a camp towel to wipe dew off surfaces before packing. Try not to pack wet gear, as it adds too much weight and may quickly get moldy. Have the next day's hiking agenda reviewed and agreed upon. Rinse out any clothing that needs it so it will dry overnight or hang it on your pack while you hike to sun-dry and gather the scents of the hemlocks or jasmine. Make sure you check your feet for problems and take appropriate action; a rubdown with wintergreen alcohol rub is great. Don't neglect your feet. If you are "normal," morning coffee is a must. Clean up, and leave camp better than it was when you got there.
- *Storing food*: If you are in bear country, this means hanging a bear bag or canister. Many shelters have strings from which a stuff sack or most likely a plastic grocery bag can be hung. Although mice are the biggest threat to your chow, if the trail telegraphs that bears are out and about, start slinging edibles and "smellables" (like toothpaste) over a tree limb, anticipating very intelligent and persistent bears. Two ropes are necessary: one to get the load up and secured, and the other to pull it away from the trunk toward an isolated piece of space at least 10 feet or so in the air. And, by the way, don't cook where you sleep. Certainly, don't take open food containers in your tent. A mouse can chew his way through oak; a freeze-dried pack is less than a minor irritant for them. These are not the cute creatures that helped Cinderella. And, finally, don't leave anything edible in your pack on the ground unprotected overnight. I found bringing my pack inside my tent did the trick—that is, if it wasn't bear country. Thankfully, bears are rarely seen; they are quite shy.
- *Camp activities*: Be prepared for journaling, reading, cards, four-part harmonies and whatever else is of interest. If you have always wanted to journal, hiking is the best, if not the only, time to begin the habit. You have the time and inspiration; just muster the discipline

to make a few notes every night at least. Even if you don't keep it up, you will have the narrative for the pictures, if not the seeds of the whoppers to come. There is just too much to recall after the fact, and that confrontation with the trail dog that nearly licks you to death may become the next great novel. Who's to say? And if you ever wanted to *stop* a habit—say, smoking, drinking, compulsive shopping, binge reruns, biting your fingernails . . . what can I say? Hiking is all-consuming, a real change from the routine back home, and a time when bad habits are not appropriate.

- *Camp etiquette*: Maintain some decorum, at least until your hiking crew proves there is no need to. This is a key to still being friends after the hike and beyond. Learn their peculiarities—everyone has one or two—and then honor them. Don't wonder about something because it may be a bit sensitive or personal; ask, speak your mind and come to an understanding. Etiquette also extends to the campsite: Be nice to the folks who follow either today or tomorrow. The Boy Scouts have it right; leave a campsite in *better* shape than when you found it.

Tip 8: Practice Good Safety, Health and Hygiene

- *Safety*: Sprained wrists are one of the biggest reasons for curtailing a backpacking trip. Banged-up upper-body limbs due to losing your footing take more people off the trail than anything else. If you hike, you *will* slip, slide, stumble and especially fall. Even though instincts take over when you hit the deck, when you fall, try to roll onto your back to let your pack take the blow. That way, all you risk are a few smashed crackers.

  Be cautious when the trail demands it. This is one of the best reasons to take hiking poles—good ones. You can add many miles to your day if distance is the goal. At the very least, you will be safer through their use. Practice with them until they become extensions of your limbs. Use them to pull yourself uphill, take the pressure off your knees and hips going downhill, and assist your gait with your arms on the straightaway. They are most helpful traversing a wet and slimy trail, especially when going over exposed roots (the main cause of slipping and crashing), and over, around and down rocks. And speaking of avoiding falls, a good deterrent to a bad fall is a trail partner with enough common sense to keep the pace humane and who knows what to do and especially *how* to do it in an emergency. Inevitably, you will be farthest from help when it is needed, and it is no fun hiking four more hours down the same rocky trail that broke your right hand: swollen, black and blue on both sides, and unable to grip a pole. Do you hear the voice of experience here?

- *Hygiene*: No matter how you slice it, visiting the thunder tree is not fun; we have been rightly spoiled by the porcelain convenience. For men, let's face it: Things are simpler in the woods. There is no need to belabor this point. After discussing the topic, delicately, with women, we are assured that dropping back on the trail for a little privacy quickly becomes routine. Naturally, women need to be prepared to pack in and out any non-biodegradable feminine hygiene products.
- *Foot care*: Finish all the camp chores, set up the tent, fetch water, clean up and then take off that heavy footgear. Put on the ol' camp shoes; I repeat, do *not* take flip-flops. Crocs with a back strap are best. They are light, and the straps keep them from floating away in a moving stream. Keeping feet clean and inspected for potential hot spots, wayward calluses and blisters is very important. Without good feet, there will be no good hike—or a hike at all.
- *First aid*: It will behoove you to learn a little first aid (see "Resources" or Google it). That way, whether it's a warm spot on your heel or a minor abrasion, you will know what to do. Consider taking a large, perhaps prescription dose of ibuprofen (or whatever preventive pain remedy suits you) in the morning and evening with food for the first few days when you may have aches, pains and sore muscles from hiking. If you do this, you will need more water, so drink up, even though you may think you have had enough. Also, as stated previously, too much ibuprofen can cause stomach ulcers with dire possibilities, so be cautious. At the earliest indication of any problem, stop the show and attend to it.

- *Hazards*: There are other hazards such as hypothermia, heat exhaustion, sprains, blisters, burns (sun and fire), too much weight, falling and stupidity, such as laying duct tape directly on a blister and leaving it there for a fortnight (yes, that was witnessed also—not pretty when the tape had to come off, with some of the hiker, too). If you hike long enough, someone will try duct tape as an easy blister fix, just to see what happens or because he's just too lazy to tend to the problem properly. Word to the wise: You may not want to be on the trail with this guy. He (it is inevitably a he) most likely will say some variation of: "Hey, hold my beer—watch this."
- *Personal health and medical record/profile*: It's advisable to have a current physical and fill out a health/medical form for trail emergencies (refer to Appendix 2). A copy of your medical insurance, blood type and contact information should be kept with your first aid kit. Make sure you share this information and its location with your partner and the person who is your emergency contact. Discuss any individual medical needs you may have. You may want to consider an ID bracelet, with your emergency contact info, allergies and current medications engraved on the band. Also, put the ICE (in case of emergency) contacts in your cell phone.

Tip 9: Have a Plan B
Even if you are anticipating only an overnighter, have an exit plan in the event things don't go per plan. You may get to that well-recommended campsite, and it is just not what you anticipated. Someone may get sick in transit. Or, heaven forbid, someone may twist an ankle. Certainly, on a longer hike, have a plan to send someone back home or arrange for transportation to have a fellow hiker taken to the next way place. Who knows, a hiking partner may have had enough hiking for a day or two and would be perfectly happy going on ahead if they can catch a bus or bum a ride.
- *Identifying possible exit sites*: Make sure during the planning stage that you know where possible exit sites are. An exit site is a place where you can get transportation back to the trailhead and a waiting car where you began the trip, should you have to end

your hike unexpectedly.
- *Exit procedures*: Often, there is someone who will take you back to the trailhead for a fee, or you can call your previously arranged shuttle if you unexpectedly need to leave the trail. If it is a trail of any popularity, there are people who will ferry or taxi you just about anywhere you wish to go. Just inquire at a gas station or convenience store, or even knock on a door. If you have made the decision to quit or it was made for you by some misfortune, it will be a relief to spend the money, and then marvel at how little time, sometimes a matter of minutes, it takes to retrace what probably took you many days or more to hike.

General Colin Powell observed that it is counterproductive to attempt to discover 100 percent of the facts, because that delay invariably leads to "analysis paralysis." He made his decisions when there was mutual agreement, a feeling that between 40 to 70 percent of the information was in hand. There comes a time when only action will do, as data needs to be tested with a dose of reality. Talk to other people, read, and hop on the internet for any question that pops up. Anticipation is part of the experience, but don't let the process of getting ready be an end in itself; schedule a departure day, call the checklist done and give it a go.

One of the great things about hiking as a boomer is you are demonstrating there are a lot of meaningful things left to do with the short rows of life. Ben Franklin thought a lot about the short rows—and did something about it. But before we get to that, let's bring our C2C hike to an end with a continuation of tales from the trail.

Coming across the North York Moors

STAGE 12: CLAY BANK TOP TO GLAISDALE

The routine of going into a town was . . . routine. We chatted with the host or hostess and asked the usual questions about what there was to see and do, and where was the best place to eat. Room arrangements for three were decided. Perhaps we had tea and a sweet as a reward for the day's work, but we enjoyed a shower or bath first. Usually, it was just a hot shower. If there was a bath, it was festooned with every imaginable bath product. Why not have bubbles—no one was looking—pour in that salty-looking stuff, then soak and luxuriate in the warmth? After cleanup, we usually headed off to the pub.

The Maltkin B&B in Clay Bank Top was the only game at this stop, in what was not a town—or at least we did not see one. So, we atypically just hung around the house chatting about the day and anything else that came to mind when reality was on the other side of the world.

We were joined by Katherine and Yvonne, which made for good conversation and a very pleasant time; they stayed in the "pig barn," which had been converted into a room. Dinner was three courses, naturally, which extended for a couple of hours in what seemed like a matter of minutes, as we were drawn in by the best of British conversation and hospitality.

The following day, we set out to the North York Moors,[18] famous, at least to me, for the miles of spectacular heather (see picture on page 147). The moors were also where wind whipped up the rain so much that it stung the face a bit. A hiking pole that dangled off my wrist was blown nearly horizontal. We were in full raingear, including good gloves, layers, rain pants and a woolly hat. The hiking was invigorating but not for the timid. Yvonne and Katherine set a mean pace. They were experienced hikers and charming to watch. Katherine had two hiking poles that she used like walking canes, with palms down instead of using them as designed—slung on the wrists like extensions of the arms. She wouldn't hear of using them as ski poles—the natural and more efficient manner. But how could we disagree? She hiked the UK and Europe for decades.

The Ashley House B&B in Glaisdale was a very nice and orderly home, since it didn't have the nearly uncountable wall hangings and knickknacks usually found in the homes at which we stayed. The lady of the house is generally the one who works with the guests and runs the inn. Occasionally, we might meet the gentleman of the house, who usually cooks the breakfast or serves dinner. Keeping these B&Bs seems to be the providence of very industrious, frugal women. The trip would not have been nearly as nice without this hospitable arrangement. I am sold on B&Bs.

Chris and I struck out for Robin Hood's Bay after another most pleasant breakfast and conversation. The bus delivered Wes there already.

---

18 http://www.northyorkmoors.org.uk/

CHAPTER 10
Correcting Errata

I took a walk in the woods and came out taller than the trees.
—Henry David Thoreau

A blaze that marks the Appalachian Trail

Since we have the older hiker very much in mind, there is another aspect of how we view what we do. For many of us, we are aware that we have more birthdays behind us than ahead, while still wanting to continue to make a bit of a difference and have a little fun along the way. Perhaps it is about giving back, leaving a place a little better for our having passed, even if it is only in the ready smile you may have put on the face of a child. We have the resources and, most important, the frame of mind to justify our consumption of those resources and generally how we pass through this life. Even the contemplation of experiencing things in their natural state, by breathing air at 6,000 feet or higher, makes us pause to consider what can be done to make sure others can have the same opportunity, if they want. We were pleasantly surprised when entering this interesting lifestyle that many folks, usually the boomers, were actively involved in good works to do with the community and the trail, if only to practice leave no trace. But there can be much more; there is much more.

You don't even have to look for it. It is there when preparing for a hike, it is on the trail, and it is certainly there after the hike, even though much more will be contemplated by being close to nature, undistracted, with the opportunity to think and breathe deeply. It must be that experiencing some sublime moments in the company of close, close friends, where the best foot forward is to achieve something, gives pause and motivation to be a good steward of our little part at the top of the food chain. And it just plain feels good to do good stuff with good people. Now, don't get this point wrong: We are *not* talking about leading revolutions and preventing mass extinctions; we are talking about simple actions that can be worked into busy, demanding, vital lives.

What is neat is that once you are into a hike or two, opportunities for good stewardship stream by whether you are on the trail or not. There is always an opportunity to clear the leaves and branches off the local nature trail. The major trails, like the AT, always need a hand, as the woods are at work 24 hours a day reclaiming the trail.

It is a great privilege and opportunity (dosed with some luck) to be on the short rows of life. We can leave the world in a little better shape, even if it is only by reading to a senior citizen once a week; who can't do that? Friends, family, fun; we as boomers are poised to push the boundaries of aging as we have done with so many other limits we have encountered.

My boomer friends ask, "Is that all there is?" after a career or two. The answer is "No!" I have made it a point to ask members of the Greatest Generation—mostly women, as the men are gone—"What is your advice for living a life worth living?" These are women who have seen and done it all, and most of it was brutal, marked by depression (personal and national), serious diseases, rotten health, war, the death of children, endless work, disappointments galore and the betrayal of false friends. And yet those I chatted with were cheerful, fun-loving and encouraging. A family friend of more than 60 years, Ma Kren, now passed on, simply said when asked that question, "Have *fun*!" What she meant is that we have probably been responsible people by getting an education, obeying the laws, slogging through careers, keeping a marriage together, raising children and the like, so we had to say "no" to so much that makes life a little more interesting, fun, accomplished and worthy, if not significant.

I personally said no to nearly all true vacations during two careers over 45 years. I am not saying that being responsible is not an accomplishment; giving the world the gift of a capable child is a remarkable achievement. I am saying that we boomers can expect to be vital, some of us to 100. We can make retirement a full-time career. We can experiment with life all over again. So, say "yes!" Learn to fly fish and teach a grandchild how to tie a small bug, then take her to the local bluegill pond. Make an apple pie together. Take up quilting and have that grandchild help. Help a good citizen get on the town council. Go on safari with the love of your life. Stand on a mountaintop and watch the eagles soar below you. Teach the next generation how to do this thing called life. Be an interesting person who gathers other interesting people around them. Having a friend and being a friend takes work. Get inspiration; be inspiration.

I personally enjoy—love, really—reading about the greats. How did they do it all, many of them in relatively brief lives? Ben Franklin is a fascinating character to wonder about and learn from, aside from the fact that he is one of the most significant people in all human history, probably one of the 100 that matter the most. As he reminisced how his life was entering the short rows, while he was still helping to win the Revolution, he pondered that he needed time to "correct errata." Here is a man who invented or reinvented the post office, public education, universities, fire departments and banking; who was an inventor, politician, author, diplomat and orator. He was a genius and *the* man for the times. It can be successfully argued that his work on electricity accelerated the advent of the Information Age; even this laptop on which I am working traces back to that kite and key on a stormy, lightning-filled night. Yet he was concerned he did not get *it*, this thing called life.

I've thought that if ol' Ben was concerned with getting things right, perhaps I should be also. It is desperately tough to live without regrets; those who say they have stretch things a bit. It is just about impossible to get through life without real troubles. I maintain that we boomers who have been pushing development in this great country since we were conceived have yet to write our greatest accomplishments, individually, and especially collectively. Even the most modest of us can do philanthropy. How will you be remembered? Consider the next generation.

There is nothing like taking a child on the trail. Make sure they have their own pack and hiking stick and watch the magic, even if the hike is only a hundred yards from the parking lot to a stream. Heaven forbid if there is a marshmallow or two to be had for the fire! It is difficult enough to find things to do as a family with the demands of career, children, preparing for retirement and all else this life entails. Getting into nature with friends, family and especially young children is magical. Children especially soak up the experience. There will be many an opportunity to say or do something that will change the life of that child for the better. How will you correct your errata?

> *Tell me and I forget, teach me and I remember,*
> *show me and I learn.*
> — Confucian philosopher Xunzi

With Warmest Regards,
The Honest Backpacker

More hikin' buddies—sheep are everywhere

STAGE 13: GROSMONT TO ROBIN HOOD'S BAY

It was a glorious hiking day through the moors. Soon we were in sight of the North Sea and lost sight of the trail. Even with Chris' excellent step-by-step navigation, we got miserably lost and had to ask where we were. Naturally, the locals knew all about the Coast-to-Coast trail and pointed us in the general direction. We deciphered the landmark that was supposed to be a camper trailer park, but there were two of them, so which one? This wouldn't usually be a problem, but when you are on foot, you are conscious of every extra step to get there from here.

We ended up going down rows of winter wheat, trying not to crush any stalks. There was absolutely no trail, so we plunged into a swale cut by a small stream. There was stinging nettle everywhere. The barbed wire was taut and high. The day was getting long. At least we had arrived at the correct camper park and were nearing the end. The Stedman guidebook demanded we follow along the water's edge. We asked a young lad if the abandoned rail bed, now a public footpath, was a bit better for our purposes; in other words, was it shorter? By now, my feet had had it. The boots, especially the left one, had done a thorough assault on my feet, which were nearly fatal to the hike. I pushed on, but if the trip were any longer, I would not have made it without a day or two of healing.

Still, it was bearable: The trip was ending, and the views of a picturesque town with hundreds of years of history and the English coast dipping into the North Sea were awe-inspiring. The day was bright and cool, and we were in England with just about everything going right.

The hike ended as it began: most pleasantly, with more hospitality and feasts for the belly and eyes. At the B&B, there was a card for all of us from our friend Caroline, congratulating us on finishing. My sore feet, victims of ill-fitting boots, took all motivation out of the ceremony of finding and putting a stone from the Irish Sea onto the cairn of stones in the North Sea, signifying yet another completed trek. We settled for dipping our boots in the North Sea. I still keep stones from each end of the trip on my bookshelf, another "trophy" of the philosophy of living a life worth living.

AFTERWORD
Perspectives of an Experienced Hiker

You will get all sorts of advice when bellying up to this kind of adventure, much of it good. When you set out, remember that everyone "hikes their own hike." This means that in addition to being a good teammate and facilitating communal decisions, each hiker needs to make personal decisions every step of the way, before, during and after the experience. Naturally, choose your own food, clothing and equipment, although the first trip will have you whittling down selections to a standard few things, where only the brand name of the item changes or dietary issues dictate a different choice. You will get into your own rhythm for trudging on, taking breaks and camping routines. Remember to debrief after the trip, to inventory your equipment, to add and subtract and use as experience dictates. Your future self will thank you. This experience is like "You say potato, I say potahto." The trail is the best teacher; we all learn from it.

The hike is a fluid thing and should grow organically; each lesson and insight grows from the previous one. A plan is good, but the trail and your reaction to it before, along the way and after will determine everything from when to get up in the morning, how far to hike, where to stay for the evening, even how many days the hike lasts and where you end up. Plan well, and be flexible as the trail unfolds. The lesson is to prepare enough, hike wisely enough and be flexible enough to make the trip an enjoyable one about which you will want to tell and retell all its stories. People are genuinely in awe to learn that we hiked across England and are enthralled by a story or two.

In all our travels, we have been a bit surprised, if not reassured, by how casual experienced hikers are. They have their minds right and their bodies in shape. They work on it. They are realistic about the rigors of being outdoors and laboring under a cumbersome pack day in and day out. They are confident in their knowledge and abilities to cope with any obstacle. They have what a novice would call Spartan packs but are complete, comfy and well-fed. They always have water and make it safe to drink by purifying or filtering it. The most common grocery items keep them fueled. Getting wet (in the summer) is OK; they know it is a probability, but they also know that they will dry out, that their socks are always dry, and that their sleeping bag is well-protected. They don't fret over where they will stay, but they do plan for shelter or a hostel. They know not to pitch their tent under a rotten tree limb. When injured, they are prepared to take a break from the hike for a few days to heal because they know they have the discipline to get back on the trail. They are confident they are becoming better people. And they have fun, making memories most folks can't even imagine.

APPENDIX 1
Leave No Trace: Outdoor Ethics

I find it satisfying to leave a campsite in better shape than when I found it, and practicing leave no trace ethics requires such a small effort to help the next traveler have a good experience. What a pleasure it is to arrive at a campsite that is in good order and completely clean, ready to make camp and have a well-deserved meal. Leave no trace[19] is all about respect for wildlife, for those who follow, and for nature. And all it takes is a little planning. The following tips from the Leave No Trace Center for Outdoor Ethics will help you conduct a no-impact hike.

Plan and Prepare[20]
- Know the regulations and special concerns for the area you'll visit. For example, you may be traveling during a dry season when the fire hazard is high, which means you may not want to light any campfires.
- Prepare for extreme weather, hazards and emergencies.
- Schedule your trip to avoid times of high use.
- Visit in small groups. Split larger parties into groups of four to six.
- Repackage food to minimize waste.
- Use a map and compass to eliminate the use of rock cairns, flagging or marking paint.

Travel and Camp on Durable Surfaces
- Stay on durable surfaces, which include established trails and campsites, rock, gravel, dry grasses, or snow.
- Protect riparian areas by camping at least 200 feet from lakes and streams.
- Good campsites are found, not made. Altering a site is not necessary in popular areas.

---
19 https://lnt.org/
20 A special thanks to Subaru for supporting and publicizing leave no trace. https://lnt.org/about/traveling-teams.

- Concentrate use on existing trails and campsites.
- Walk single file in the middle of the trail, even when wet or muddy.
- Keep campsites small. Focus activity in areas where vegetation is absent in pristine areas.
- Disperse use to prevent the creation of campsites and trails. If campsites are not pre-designated, try not to overuse one area if you can, as the primo sites will be obvious. Go a little farther to see if there is another agreeable spot.
- Avoid places where the area is just beginning to be impacted by human traffic and use.

Dispose of Waste Properly
- Pack it in, pack it out. Inspect your campsite and rest areas for trash or spilled foods. Pack out all trash, leftover food and litter.
- Deposit solid human waste in cat holes dug 6 to 8 inches deep and at least 200 feet from water, campsites and trails. Cover and disguise the cat hole when finished.
- Pack out toilet paper and hygiene products.
- To wash yourself or your dishes, carry water 200 feet away from streams or lakes and use small amounts of biodegradable soap. Scatter strained dishwater.

Leave What You Find
- Preserve the past: Examine, but do not touch, cultural or historic structures and artifacts.
- Leave rocks, plants and other natural objects as you found them.
- Avoid introducing or transporting non-native species.
- Do not build structures or furniture or dig trenches.

Minimize Campfire Impact
Campfires can cause a lasting impact on the backcountry. Fires have a way of carving out a goodly hunk of ground and invite continuous use, which means the surrounding area will be stripped of anything that burns and more. A fire pit tends to collect garbage and, horrors, beer cans. It ceases to be natural.

- Use a lightweight stove for cooking, and enjoy a candle lantern or battery headlamp for light.
- Where fires are permitted, use established fire rings, fire pans or mound fires.
- Keep fires small. Only use sticks from the ground that can be broken by hand.
- Burn all wood and coals to ash; put out campfires completely, then scatter cool ashes.

Respect Wildlife
- Observe wildlife from a distance. Do not follow or approach them. Never feed animals. Feeding wildlife damages their health, alters natural behaviors, and exposes them to predators and other dangers.
- Protect wildlife and your food by storing rations and trash securely.
- Control pets always, or leave them at home.
- Avoid wildlife during sensitive times: mating, nesting, raising young or winter.

Be Considerate of Other Visitors
- Respect other visitors and protect the quality of their experience.
- Be courteous. Yield to other users on the trail.
- Step to the downhill side of the trail when encountering pack stock.
- Take breaks and camp away from trails and other visitors.
- Let nature's sounds prevail. Avoid loud voices and noises.

APPENDIX 2
Adult Medical Information for the Trail

*Take this form on the trail with you,
and keep it with your first aid kit.*

Given Name(s): _____ Surname: _____

Address: _____

_____

_____

Phone:
Home: _____ Business: _____ Mobile: _____

Email: _____

Date of Birth: _____

Emergency Contact: _____ Relationship: _____

Phone:
Home: _____ Business: _____ Mobile: _____

Email: _____

Health Insurance Company: _____ Plan ID: _____

Regular Doctor or Clinic: _____ Phone: _____

Are you presently taking medications? Yes/No If yes, what type and dosage? _____

_____

_____

Detail any medical or physical condition that could affect this trip: _____

_____

_____

_____

Detail any significant injury, operation or illness during the last 12 months: ___

_____

_____

Allergies: _____

Date of last tetanus immunization: _____

The above detail is an accurate indication of my present medical status, and I will modify the above details before this event if necessary.

Signature: _____ Date: _____

APPENDIX 3
Authorization and Consent Form

(Confidential and to be used only in case of emergency)

Name:_____ County: _____

Event:_____ Location of event: _____

County/State: _____ Dates: To: _____ From: _____

I hereby certify that I am in good health and can travel to and participate in this event.

While I am attending, or traveling to or from this function, I hereby authorize the adults in my event crew, or in their absence or disability, any adult accompanying or assisting them, to consent to the following medical treatment for me should I be unable to make a decision:

> Any X-ray examination, anesthetic, medical, or surgical diagnosis or treatment; and hospital care that is deemed advisable by, and is to be rendered under the general or special supervision of any licensed physician and/or surgeon; or any X-ray examination, anesthetic, dental, or surgical diagnosis or treatment; and hospital care to be rendered by a licensed dentist.

Authorization and Consent

Date:_____ Signature: _____

In the event of an emergency, please contact: _____

Address: _____

_____

Daytime Phone:_____ Evening: _____

Non-Consent

I do not desire to sign this authorization and understand that this will prohibit my receiving any medical attention in the event of illness or accident.

Date:_____ Signature: _____

This document is only valid during participation in the following event:

_____

APPENDIX 4
Adult Medical History

Bring this form with you on a visit to your medical provider, or they can supply you with a similar one.

Name: _____ Date of Birth: _____ Current Age: _____

Are you subject to:	Yes	No	Do you now have or have you ever had:	Yes	No
Colds			Heart trouble		
Sore throat			Asthma		
Fainting spells			Lung trouble		
Bronchitis			Sinus trouble		
Convulsions			Hernia (rupture)		
Cramps			Appendicitis		
Allergies			Has your appendix been removed?		
Is your eyesight good?			Do you walk in your sleep?		
Is your hearing good?			Are you under medical care?		
Explain any yes items:					
Explain any history of behavior disorders or treatment for emotional disturbance:					

Please identify your allergies, including allergies to food, medications or drug reactions you know of:
_____
_____

Please list any physical disabilities or disorders that may affect your participation at this function, such as eyesight, hearing, speech, paralysis, diabetes, ulcers, etc.:
_____
_____

Please list all medications you are presently taking:

    Name of Medication: Dosage: Times Taken:
_____
_____

Remarks and/or any special instructions: _____
_____

Resources

In keeping with the practical nature of this view of backpacking for the mature hiker, references are redundant. I contemplated for a moment not even suggesting references, since there is so much available at the click of a mouse and the preparation for an experience of any nature is different for every person. I hope this missive is the motivation to spark real creativity on what you can do to live a life worth living. If I have motivated you, nay, inspired you to dream with *The Honest Backpacker*, then I will have succeeded. So, plow on and let the internet and your heart lead you to the most wondrous places.

Spend a little time on the internet, and you will find an abundance of good material. However, if you have the time, inclination and budget, some of the best information, if not *the* best, is given at the Appalachian Trail Conservancy, and will apply to just about any hike or outdoors experience. A trip to the bookstore or library will also fulfill your research needs. Take your pick of the titles listed below or what fills in the holes in your level of expertise and needs. Perhaps it is best to buy a few of the books that strike your fancy, as you may want to digest them with a highlighter and pencil. Besides, they are nice additions to any library. You could also look into outfitters, especially those who specialize in your location of interest; they will offer plenty of advice, literature, maps, instructions and classes.

The trick is to be choosy about what to read and save, and not let yourself become overwhelmed. A good rule of thumb is to simply prepare and research the best you can, until you can say, "I have done what is reasonable; if I have missed something, it won't be much, it's OK. I'll figure it out on the trail, if necessary." Then do it. Go hiking, adjust, and do it again. Study must end and action must begin to really learn. In fact, the learning curve of that first trip is one of the biggest you will ever experience. Another rule of thumb is to do enough to be ready enough for that first trip so it does not turn you off to the pleasures of further adventures. And that first trip need only be an overnighter to the local park or to a favorite fishing hole with your son or daughter.

Books and Periodicals

There are loads of backpacking resources in bookstores and on the internet, so this list is mercifully brief and to the point. But you will find, as we did, that there is a dearth of information on the specific needs of a mature boomer hiker, since we need a more comprehensive approach to going on an adventure. So, buy or download what augments *The Honest Backpacker*. One of the themes of *The Honest Backpacker* is to be a point of departure, so this list is meant to be the impetus for you to build your own references.

Here are a few that have proved particularly helpful to us over time, for reasons made obvious by their titles and contents.

> Curtis, Rick. *The Backpacker's Field Manual: A Comprehensive Guide to Mastering Backcountry Skills.* (Three Rivers Press, 2005). This is a comprehensive, 347-page reference from the director of Princeton University's Outdoor Action Program, which targets the wilderness adventurer. The program's website (https://outdooraction.princeton.edu/) is among the most helpful online resources for backpacking besides the book, which is at: http://backpackersfieldmanual.com/.

> Daoust, Gene and Daoust, Joyce. *The Formula: A Personalized 40-30-30 Weight Loss Program.* (New York: Ballantine Books, 2001). While much of the book promotes a line of food supplements, its value lies in the variety of lean meals recommended for shedding a few pounds and toning up for the rigors of leaving your computer, cubicle and couch.

> Hall, Adrienne. *Backpacking: A Woman's Guide.* (Camden, ME: Ragged Mountain Press, 1998). This is a short book on the basics of backpacking. There are a few comments on what "necessaries" must be done in the woods, which take a bit of getting used to, no

matter who you are. The resource directory is quite good.

Logue, Victoria and Logue, Frank. *The Appalachian Trail Backpacker: Trail-Proven Advice for Hikes of Any Length.* (Birmingham, AL: Menasha Ridge Press, 2001). This is a book of good tips in general and specifically for gear. It is focused on the Appalachian Trail, which is a good proving ground for just about any hike.

McManners, Hugh. *The Backpacker's Handbook* (DK Adult, 1995). McManners touches on a lot in this effectively illustrated 160-page book. Designed to fit in your pack, it covers everything from packing for a long trip to body and hand gestures recognized in foreign lands.

Phillips, Bill. *Body for Life: 12 Weeks to Mental and Physical Strength.* (New York: Harper Collins, 1999). This book is another momentarily popular book on fitness; much of it is devoted to advertising the author's supplements. The value of the book lies in the relatively few pages devoted to how a workout should be done. It is most sensible and rooted in the training routines done by Olympians.

Roizen, Michael. *RealAge: Are You as Young as You Can Be?* (New York: Harper Collins, 1999). Dr. Roizen factors in more than 100 separate behaviors to determine your real, not your chronological, age. Simple things—most are obvious but some are not—make a big difference in helping the body remain as efficient and effective as possible as it grows older. The good advice is written for the everyday reader.

Stedman, Henry. *Coast to Coast Path: British Walking Guide: Planning, Places to Stay, Places to Eat.* (Trailblazer Publications, Surry, UK. 6th ed.). "Fully revised 6th edition of this classic 191-mile walk across northern England from the

Irish Sea to the North Sea, inspired by Alfred Wainwright. Crossing three fabulous national parks—the Lake District, the Yorkshire Dales, and the North York Moors—it samples the very best of the English countryside—rugged mountains and lakes, gentle dales and stone-built villages; wild moorland; sea cliffs and fishing villages. Six town plans and 109 large-scale walking maps showing route times, places to stay, places to eat, points of interest and much more. These maps are fully edited maps drawn by walkers for walkers. There are itineraries for all walkers—whether walking the route in its entirety over two weeks or sampling the highlights on day walks and short breaks. Practical information for all budgets—camping, bunkhouses, hostels, B&Bs, pubs and hotels; St Bees through to Robin Hood's Bay—where to stay, where to eat, what to see, plus detailed street plans. Comprehensive public transport information—for all access points on the Coast to Coast. Path flora and fauna—four-page full-color flower guide, plus an illustrated section on local wildlife. Green hiking—understanding the local environment and minimizing our impact on it."[21]

Websites

A Ton of Tips for the Aspiring Appalachian Trail Hiker: A Close Look at Gear, Technique and Attitude, Paul Comstock. A quick and very informative read. www.gallifrey.org/AT1.html

Appalachian Trail Conservancy. This is a great example of the resources available on a national, if not internationally renowned, hike. It is a great general resource as a suggestion for what to look for about a hike from advocacy to volunteering and beyond, no matter what experience you are contemplating. www.appalachiantrail.org/

Building a Hiker's First Aid Kit. A first aid kit is one of the 10 essentials you should always take on a hike, and it's especially

---

[21] Extracted from the Barnes and Noble website: http://www.barnesandnoble.com/w/coast-to-coast-path-henry-stedman/1120178151.

important on an overnight backpacking trip. You'll use some of the contents regularly and should replace those often (moleskin for blisters, bandages and aspirin), while others will be rarely used but are critical in an emergency. Each person's kit should vary, depending on the medical conditions of the hikers in the party, the length and duration of the trip, and the area you'll be hiking into. http://www.wta.org/go-outside/basics/like-your-life-depends-on-it-building-your-first-aid-kit

Leave No Trace: Center for Outdoor Ethics. You should visit this if you are new to hiking and taking the next generation of hikers on the trail. There's nothing like starting off with the right frame of mind for what's natural and needs to stay that way. http://www.lnt.org

Disclaimer

This book is meant only as a guide and does not guarantee your safety in any way—you hike at your own risk. Neither Affinitas LLC nor James Klopovic is liable for property loss or damage, personal injury, or death that results in any way from accessing or hiking the trails described in this book. Be aware that hikers have been injured in these areas and while hiking in general. Be especially cautious when walking on or near boulders, steep inclines and drop-offs, and do not attempt to explore terrain that may be beyond your abilities. To help ensure an enjoyable hike, carefully read this book and thoroughly familiarize yourself with the relevant hiking regulations and areas you intend to visit before venturing: Ask questions, prepare for the unforeseen, and obtain safety information and guidance from additional resources.

The information presented in this book is in no way intended as medical advice or as a substitute for medical counseling. The information should be used in conjunction with the guidance and care of your physician or health provider. Consult your physician or health provider before beginning any exercise and nutrition program. If you choose not to obtain the consent of your physician or health provider and/or work with them throughout the duration of your time using the recommendations in this book, you are agreeing to accept full responsibility for your actions.

By continuing with the programs, exercises, advice, information or diets found here, you recognize that despite all precautions on the part of Affinitas LLC and Affinitas Publishing, there are risks of injury or illness that can occur because of your use of the aforementioned information, and you expressly assume such risks and waive, relinquish and release any claim that you may have against Affinitas LLC or its affiliates as a result of any future physical injury or illness incurred in connection with, or as a result of, use or misuse of the programs, exercises, advice, diets and/or information found in this book.

Photo Credits

Cover Photo/**Christopher Hoina Sr. Photographs**

Page III: *A view from the Coast-to-Coast hike across England, the second most popular hike in the world*/**Christopher Hoina Sr. Photographs**

Page 1: *Laurel Falls on the Appalachian Trail*/**www.nps.gov**

Page 3: *Because flowers say it all*/**www.daveallenphotography.com**

Page 11: *Any ol' stream in England—one of scores on the Coast-to-Coast hike*/**Christopher Hoina Sr. Photographs**

Page 13: *A kissing gate to keep sheep from straying on the England Coast-to-Coast hike*/**Christopher Hoina Sr. Photographs**

Page 19: *Go wherever your imagination leads you.*/**James Klopovic**

Page 32: *Ennerdale Water in England's Lake District*/**www.shutterstock.com**

Page 35: *The Irish Sea and the beginning of the England Coast-to-Coast hike along the cliff*/**Christopher Hoina Sr. Photographs**

Page 37: *Hikin' buddies: St Bees in the background on the England Coast-to-Coast*/**Christopher Hoina Sr. Photographs**

Page 43: *The suggested stops along the 192 miles of the England Coast-to-Coast hike*/**www.pietsmulders.nl**

Page 75: *It's hard to get lost on the Appalachian Trail.*/**mariafafardwrites.wordpress.com**

Page 83: *An English house on the Coast-to-Coast, probably in the family for a hundred years or more*/**Christopher Hoina Sr. Photographs**

Page 89: *All the gear for a wilderness backpacking experience*/**circlevilleherald.com**

Page 92: *How to pack a backpack*/**zombiehunters.org**

Page 98: *Bear bag*/**trailspace.com**

Page 117: *Crackerjack with English bangers and mash in stout gravy—the smile says it all*/**James Klopovic**

Page 126: *Frank's Bridge and residents of Kirkby Stephen who will gladly take any crumbs offered*/**www.visitcumbria.com**

Page 129: *Coming into Kirkby Steven*/**www.kirkbystephenhostel.co.uk**

Page 131: *The last few moments on the Coast-to-Coast*/**Christopher Hoina Sr. Photographs**

Page 147: *Coming across the New York Moors*/**inntravel.co.uk**

Page 149: *A blaze that marks the Appalachian Trail*/**Christopher Hoina Sr. Photographs**

Page 154: *More hikin' buddies—sheep are everywhere*/**commons.wikimedia.org**

About the Authors

When **Jim Klopovic** retired after two careers and 50 years of "flying a desk," he resolved to spend the best years of his life making new friends and memories and giving back. He decided to try backpacking and immediately fell in love with it. His many backpacking adventures have included hiking the England Coast-to-Coast Walk and portions of the Appalachian Trail while continuing to explore the world. Jim's motivation for writing *The Honest Backpacker* is to inspire his fellow baby boomers (and others) to stay active, take the road less traveled, and experience the wonders of the trail. He lives in Morrisville, North Carolina.

Nicole Klopovic discovered her passion for outdoor activities as a child, when her father, Jim, would take her and her sister on nature excursions around their home in North Carolina. She is an avid backpacker whose experiences include hiking above 15,000 feet to Laguna 69 in Peru's Cordillera Blanca mountain range. Her plans for future trips include hiking the Appalachian Trail and her ancestral homelands, Croatia and Australia, with her father. She lives and works as a certified physician assistant in Sacramento, California.

INDEX

Note:
Page numbers in ***bold italics*** refer to photographs or illustrations. Page numbers in ***bold italics*** followed by the letter "f" refer to forms, charts, or maps.

A

accommodations, reserving, 24, 29
Adult Medical History form, ***162f***
Adult Medical Information for the Trail form, ***160f***
age, real, 49–51
alcohol wipes, 109
anaerobic exercises, 57, 65
antibiotics, 106
antihistamines, 107
Appalachian Trail (AT), ***1***, 20–21, 24, ***75***, ***149***
Authorization and Consent Form, ***161f***

B

baby boomers, 3–4, 6
Backpacker's Field Manual, The (Curtis), 76
backpacking classes, 24–25
backpacks, 25, 92–93, ***92***. *See also* gear; packing
backup leaders, 138
baggies, 93
balance training, 62–63
bandages, 105, 107
bandannas, 104
bear bags, 93, 98–99, ***98***, 142
Benadryl, 107
benefits of hiking, 7–10
blisters, 26, 106, 112, 144, 145
Body for Life (Phillips), 60–61
boomer generation, 3–4, 6
bottles, 99–100, 123
breakfast foods, 123
breaking camp, 142
breathing while exercising, 66–67
brushes, 109
burn ointments, 107

C

cameras, 113
camp activities, 112–113, 142
camp equipment. *See* gear; packing
camp etiquette, 143. *See also* leave-no-trace camping
camp suds, 122
camp towels, 123
campfires, 157, 158–159
campsites, 136, 157–159. *See also* leave-no-trace camping
carabiners, 99
cell phone usage, 29
checklists, 12–16, ***17f***, 28, 72, 124–125
children, hiking with, 152
cholesterol levels, 51
Clay Bank Top to Glaisdale hike, 147–148
clothing, 100–104, 112
Coast-to-Coast (C2C) hike, 6–7, ***11***, ***13***, 15, 24, 31–32, ***32***, ***35***, ***37***, ***43f***, ***83***, ***87***, 126–127, ***126***, ***129***, ***131***, 147–148, ***147***, 153–154
coffee, 124
combs, 109
compasses, 110–111, 139
cooking gear, 95–99, 122
cookpots, 97, 122
core strengthening, 56–57, 63–64
correcting errata, 40, 151–153
courtesy and respect of others, 159
CrossFit, 57–58, 67
cups, 97
cycling clubs, 61

D

daily mileage goals, 135–136
day hiking, 72
denatured stoves, 96. *See also* stoves
dental care products, 108
diarrhea remedies, 105

diet
  attitude towards, 46–52
  calorie intake and burn when hiking, 54
  daily meal schedule, 54–56
  40-30-30 plan, 52–55
  nutrition and, 24
  realistic expectations and, 40
  three simple rules, 45
  whole person approach and, 71
dinner foods, 124
dishwashing supplies, 122
duct tape, 108

E
emergencies, 78
endurance, increasing, 57
England Coast-to-Coast (C2C) hike, 6–7, *11*, *13*, 15, 24, 31–32, *32*, *35*, *37*, *43f*, *83*, *87*, 126–127, *126*, *129*, *131*, 147–148, *147*, 153–154
enjoyment vs. timetable, 132, 138
equipment. *See* gear
ethics of camping, 77, 108, 136, 141, 143, 157–159. *See also* stewardship of trails
etiquette, camp, 143. *See also* leave-no-trace camping
exercises
  aerobic, 57, 64
  alternating, benefit of, 67–68
  anaerobic, 57, 65
  balance, 62–63
  flexibility, 56–57, 62–63
  high intensity interval training, 57
  resistance, 57, 65–67
  whole person approach and, 71–72
exercising. *See also* physical conditioning
  apps for, 58
  breathing while, 66–67
  dealing with setbacks, 69–70
  having realistic expectations, 69
  making it a habit, 59–60
  routines, 58
  starting slow, 56
  stretching and, 62, 68
  types of, 56–59
  varying, 58, 61
  weekly workout, 68–69
exit sites and procedures, 145–146

expectations, setting, 40–41
experienced hikers, 155–156

F
family and friends, staying in touch with, 30
feminine hygiene products, 107, 109
first aid, 26, 78, 106, 144
first aid supplies, 105–107
fitness, mental, 75–79
fitness, physical, 5, 23–24, 26–27, 38–39, 41–42, 47. *See also* diet; exercising
flexibility exercises, 56–57, 62–63
food
  breakfast, 123
  dinner, 124
  eating regularly, 140
  gear for preparing, 122–123
  handling, 140
  lunch, 124
  menu planning, 54–56, 119–120, *119f*, 140
  nutritious, 120–121
  personal nutrition requirements and, 77
  perspective and, 118–119
  procuring, 27
  resupplying along the way, 140
  storing, 93, 98–99, *98*, 142
  tents and, 142
foot care, 26, 101, 106, 137, 144
Formula: A Personalized 40-30-30 Weight Loss Program, The (Daoust and Daoust), 52–55
40-30-30 plan, 52–55
Franklin, Benjamin, 9, 40, 47, 130, 151
fry pans, 97–98, 122
fuel, 96, 122
full-body workout, weekly, 68–69

G
gaiters, 104
gauze, 107
gear, *89*. *See also* food; packing
  adjusting, 137
  backpacks, 25, 92–93, *92*
  bear bags, 98–99, *98*, 142
  buying, 90–91, 133
  cameras, 113
  camp activities, 112–113, 142

Index

carabiners, 99
  clothing, 100–104, 112
  cooking, 95–98, 122
  duct tape, 108
  familiarizing yourself with, 77
  first aid, 105–107
  fuel, 96, 122
  gloves, 112
  headlamps, 108
  hiking poles, 26, 72, 112, 143–144, 148
  hydration, 99–100, 123
  lighters, 96–97
  moisture barriers, 94
  orienteering, 77–78, 110–111, 138–139
  pocketknives, 107–108
  ropes, 99
  sleeping, 93–95
  stoves, 26, 95–97, 122, 159
  tents, 26, 73, 93–94, 97, 108, 142
  toiletries, 108–109
getting it right, 40, 151–153
giving back, 130
gloves, 112
Grosmont to Robin Hood's Bay hike, 153–154
gyms, joining, 60–61

H
hankies, 104
hats, 103
hazards, 145
headlamps, 108
health insurance, 81
healthy lifestyle, 46–52
high intensity interval training (HIIT), 57
hike reviews, 138
Hiker's Timeline of Milestones, **17f**
hikes, planning, 21–23
hiking conditions, 132–133
hiking pace and routine, 136
hiking poles, 26, 72, 112, 143–144, 148
hiking your own hike, 155
hog-snout water bags, 100
hot spots, 26, 101, 106, 137, 144
hydration, 99–100, 136–137
hydration gear, 99–100, 123
hygiene, 144

I
ibuprofen, 105
inoculations, 28
insect repellents, 106
itineraries, 30

J
jackets, 102
journaling, 9, 110, 111, 142–143

L
leaders, 138
leave-no-trace camping, 77, 108, 136, 141, 143, 157–159. *See also* stewardship of trails
Lexan spoons, 97
lifting weights, 57, 65–67
lighters, 96–97
lip balm, 106
living life, 150–151
location, orienting to, 77–78, 110–111, 138–139
long-sleeve shirts, 101–102
lost, becoming, 139. *See also* location, orienting to
lunch foods, 124

M
maps, 110, 138–139
meal planning, 54–56, 119–120, **119f**, 140
medical exams, 23, 79–81
medical information, 80, 145, **160f**, **162f**
medications, 27, 80–81, 124
meetings for planning hikes, 21–23
mental fitness, 75–79
menu planning, 54–56, 119–120, **119f**, 140
milestone timelines, 12–16, **17f**, 22
milestones
  about, 12
  attending backpacking classes, 24–25
  buying backpacks, 25
  checking weather, 29
  confirming accommodations, 29
  deciding where and when to hike, 19–20
  determining trail conditions, 29
  eating better, 24
  food procurement, 27
  hitting the trail, 30

meeting of fellow hikers, 21–23
next trip planning, 30–31
one year out: whole person plan, 71
packing, 29
personal affairs, attending to, 28–29
physical conditioning, beginning, 23–24
physical exams, 23, 79–81
planning for phone use, 29
post-trip critique, planning, 28
post-trip debriefs, conducting, 30
prescription medication procurement, 27
reserving accommodations, 24–22
shakedown trips, 26
six months out: preparation, 72
six weeks out: trail hardening, 73–74
three months out: weekly hikes, 72–73
trailhead research, 20–21
training in gear, 26
mindfulness, 39–40, 41–42
mock hikes, 59
moisture barriers, 94
money, 113

N
nail files, 107
Nalgene bottles, 99–100, 123
Neosporin, 105
next trip planning, 30–31
North York Moors, **147**
nutrition, 24, 39, 45, 120. *See also* diet; food

O
orienteering, 77–78, 110–111, 138–139
outdoor ethics, 77, 108, 136, 141, 143, 157–159. *See also* stewardship of trails

P
pack covers, 93
packing. *See also* food; gear
   about backpacks, 92–93, **92**
   adjusting gear and, 137
   baggies for, 93
   bear bag equipment, 98–99
   camp activities, 112–113
   checklists for, 124–125
   clothing, 100–104, 112
   conserving weight, 114–115
   cooking gear and fuel, 95–98
   essentials only, 133
   first aid supplies, 105–107
   hydration gear, 99–100
   journaling equipment, 111
   money, 113
   orienting gear, 110–111
   pack covers, 93
   personalizing, 124–125
   repair gear and supplies, 107–108
   suggested packing list, 89–91
   sunglasses, 103
   tent and sleeping gear, 93–95
   toiletries, 108–109
   wallets, 113–114
pans, 97–98
pants, 103
personal affairs, attending to, 28–29
phone use, 29
photography, 113
physical conditioning, 5, 23–24, 26–27, 38–39, 41–42, 47. *See also* diet; exercises; exercising
physical exams, 23, 79–81
pillows, 95
plan B, 145–146
platypus bottles, 100
pocketknives, 107–108
post-trip debriefs, 28, 30
prepaid phone cards, 29
preparation. *See also* milestones; physical conditioning
   flexibility during, 155
   gaining technical skills, 72, 76–78
   knowing when enough is enough, 79
   leaving no trace and, 157
   mental fitness and, 75–79
   overview, 14–16
   physical exams and medical fitness, 23, 79–81
   spirit, fitness of, 83–86
prescription medications, 27, 80–81, 124
purifying water, 99, 100, 136–137

R
RealAge: Are You as Young as You Can Be? (Roizen), 49–50
realistic expectations, 40–41
repair equipment, 107–108

reserving accommodations, 24, 29
resistance exercises, 57, 65–67
rest breaks, 137
ropes, 99
rubbing alcohol, 107

S
safety, 143–144
St Bees to Ennerdale Bridge hike, 31–32, *32*
setting up camp, 141
shakedown trips, 26
Shap to Kirkby Stephen hike, 126–127, *126*, *129*
shirts, 101–102
shoe inserts, 101
shoes, 101, 104
side trips, 137
sleeping gear, 93–95
sleepwear, 102–103
soap, 108–109
socks and liners, 101
spinning, 64
spirit, fitness of, 40, 83–86
sponges, 97, 123
statins, 51
stewardship of trails, 149–150. *See also* leave-no-trace camping
storing food, 93, 98–99, *98*, 142
stoves, 26, 95–97, 122, 159
street clothes, 112
stretching, 62, 68
stuff sacks, 92–93, 123
sunglasses, 103
sunscreen, 106
sweaters, 102
swim trunks, 104
swimming, 64

T
technical competence, 72, 76–78
tents, 26, 73, 93–94, 97, 108, 142
time, orienting to, 111
timelines of milestones, 12–16, 22. *See also* milestones
toilet paper, 109
toiletries, 108–109
toothpaste, 108
towels, camp, 109

trail conditions, 29
trail guides, 135
trail hardening, 73–74
trailhead research, 20–21
training in gear, 26
Trangia stoves, 96, 122. *See also* stoves
transportation to and from hike, 133–135
treadmills, 64
T-shirts, 102
Tylenol, 105

U
underwear, 102
utensils, cooking, 98, 122

V
vaccinations, 28
vitamins, 124

W
wallets, 113–114
waste disposal, 158
water bottles and bags, 99–100, 123
water purification, 99, 100, 136–137
water sites, 136–137
weather conditions, 29
weekly full-body workout, 68–69
weekly hikes, 72–73
weekly workouts, 68–69
weight conservation when packing, 114–115
whole person, 36–42, 71–72
wicking fabrics for clothing, 101–102
wilderness survival, 139
wildlife, respecting, 159
windscreens, 122
writing implements, 111

Y
yoga, 56–57, 62–63

www.ingramcontent.com/pod-product-compliance
Lightning Source LLC
Chambersburg PA
CBHW070615300426
44113CB00010B/1535